THE BACK HOME SERIES

Series Titles

At the Lake
Jim Landwehr

Wrong Tree: Adventures in Wildlife Biology
Jeffrey M. Wilson

Body Talk
Takwa Gordon

The In-Between State
Martha Lundin

North Freedom
Carolyn Dallmann

Ohio Apertures
Robert Miltner

Praise for
Jim Landwehr

"Each chapter in this book feels like its own mini-vacation. A master of detail, Landwehr takes the reader straight into rustic cabins with their knotty pine paneling, in-progress puzzles, and winged visitors in the night. We feel a part of his family, bonding over boat rides, fishing, and a beer or two. In good times and in grief, he reminds us, the small moments we spend in nature with those we love are sacred."

—Kim Suhr
author of *Nothing to Lose*
Director of Red Oak Writing

"*At the Lake* will strike a chord with any reader who's ever vacationed "up north." Jim Landwehr's memoir is a heartwarming collage of personal yet universal memories – the exhilarating leap off an old wood pier into frigid lake water, the slap of a screen door on a hot day, the bliss of landing that first fish, and the contentment of sinking into a chair on a sultry afternoon with a chilled beer in hand and the world's troubles at bay. Taken together, the stories of summers spent at the small lakeside cabins that dot the upper Midwest are a tribute to a simpler time and to the bonds of family and friendship that shape life's good times and guide us through the rough patches. A sweet read."

—Patricia Skalka
author of the Dave Cubiak *Door County Mysteries*

"Jim Landwehr's *At The Lake* takes us on a journey of Northwoods adventures. The touchstone of these memories is a trip to the quintessential 'up north' cabin, a place where families gather to build traditions and chase muskies."

—Jeff Nania
author of the award-winning *Northern Lakes Mystery Series*

AT THE LAKE

a memoir

JIM LANDWEHR

Cornerstone Press
Stevens Point, Wisconsin

Cornerstone Press, Stevens Point, Wisconsin 54481
Copyright © 2022 Jim Landwehr
www.uwsp.edu/cornerstone

Printed in the United States of America by
Point Print and Design Studio, Stevens Point, Wisconsin

Library of Congress Control Number: 2022939402
ISBN: 979-8-9861447-4-0

Cornerstone Press titles are produced in courses and internships offered by the
Department of English at the University of Wisconsin–Stevens Point.

DIRECTOR & PUBLISHER   EXECUTIVE EDITOR
Dr. Ross K. Tangedal   Jeff Snowbarger

SENIOR EDITORS
Lexie Neeley, Monica Swinick, Kala Buttke

PRESS STAFF
Rhiley Block, Alyssa Bronk, Grace Dahl, Patrick Fogarty, Ava Freeman, Angela
Green, Brett Hill, Cale Jacoby, Hunter Keisow, Adam King, Jeremy Kremser, Amanda
Leibham, Leo McEvilly, Abbi Rohde, Abbi Wasielewski

Hibbing Lake

Starting the motor
it's pull and tug the cord
and learn how to choke.

You don't have to be from the Midwest to appreciate life at the place we all know as "the cabin." These homes away from home come in all different shapes and sizes with varying degrees of amenities and inconveniences. Part of the fun of the cabin is changing up the way we live our everyday lives. Although most of these vacation hideaways are located on a lake, river, or stream, some are not. It's not a requirement, but it helps. The water element creates opportunities beyond just an ordinary cabin in the woods. But frankly, anywhere up north, away from the city in a wooded environment qualifies as a cabin, at least for me.

My first cabin experience was a place Mom and her boyfriend took us to in Hibbing, Minnesota. In 1969, a couple of years after my dad was killed, Mom started to date. She held a job as an administrative assistant at Texaco Oil. At work she met Steve, an older gentleman who took a liking to Mom and eventually asked her out. We kids only met Steve a few times, usually before the two of them went out on dates. The only things we knew about him was he worked at Texaco, and he was rich. It seemed like every time he came over to our house, he brought something for us kids.

1

As it turned out, Steve owned a cabin on a lake in Hibbing, Minnesota. In the summer of 1969, he invited all of us up for a weekend. Mom mentioned it to us kids, and naturally we were all very excited at the prospect. Of course, this was a huge undertaking if you think about getting six kids into a car for a three-hour drive, anywhere. She must have been desperate for a getaway because we packed up and went.

I was only seven years old at the time, so my memory fades on many of the details of that trip, including the name of the lake. I do remember touring an open pit mine at some point during our getaway. The city of Hibbing is in the heart of the Iron Range, so a mine tour is just one of the things you do when visiting. I remember Mom snapping a few family photos of us kids in front of a massive scoop bucket and a monstrous truck tire. These educational relics sat next to explanatory placards describing their use and dimensions. It felt like we were seeing the bigger world outside our little house back in the Twin Cities.

Something I remember with great fondness was the fishing venture my brothers and I took one morning. Tom was six years older than me and was an avid fisherman, even at his young age of thirteen. Somehow, he convinced Mom to let him take me and Rob out in Steve's boat.

We got up early and got dressed for our adventure. I guess I never gave a thought to the fact that the entire escapade was captained by a thirteen-year-old who didn't have a driver's license but was somehow cleared to run a boat. Things like that didn't deter me. All I knew was I was going fishing!

Mom's approval of this arrangement was a testament to the responsibility she placed on her two oldest children, Tom and Patty. Tom was often tasked with household repairs as well as outdoor entertainment activities with us boys. Patty was charged with altogether too many babysitting assignments, as well as keeping the house in order while Mom was at work all day. The two of them shouldered the tasks well and, in some respects, were cheated out of a bit of their own childhoods. But when tragedy like the loss of a parent hits a family, everyone from the top down was expected to rise to the challenge. It's just that more was expected of the eldest boy and girl.

Before any of us got in the boat, we put on our bright-orange Mae West life preservers. It was an obvious requirement set forth by Mom. This way she knew at a minimum, if any of us went overboard, we were at least going to float.

Tom choked the engine, pulled the ripcord a couple of times, and eventually the motor fired up. We released the dock tethers and putted out into the lake. Tom motored us out a ways near a patch of reeds and set us up with some minnows as our bait. Rob and I were clearly along as tourists on our brother's guided trip. We cast our lines, watched our bobbers, and waited. The lake was quiet and calm. Even at this young age, the peaceful and meditative qualities of being on the water spoke to my soul. This was my first time in a boat fishing with my brothers. Little did I know it would become a source of bonding for all four of us over the years, as we grew up fishing together on the lakes and rivers of Minnesota and Wisconsin. It's funny how it takes a lifetime to realize and appreciate outings like these with family. We were truly blessed to have one another.

Before long, Tom's bobber went down, and he set the hook and began his retrieve. Rob and I gawked in amazement as Tom brought in a large northern pike. Neither Rob nor I had seen a pike like this before. It was a little over 24" long and looked menacing with its deep green colors, spotted markings and alligator-like appearance. It was a truly impressive catch, especially for a thirteen-year-old.

Tom unhooked the fish, strung it and dropped the stringer over the side. There is nothing that spurs jealousy among fishermen than someone else catching one when you haven't. Rob and I fished on to try and curb that jealousy. Within an hour, my bobber bubbled under the surface as I snapped out of my lake-induced trance and started reeling in panic mode.

"I got one!" I said.

"For real?" Tom replied.

"Yeah!"

"Bring it over to the side, Jimmy."

I steered the fish to the side of the boat as I strained to catch a glimpse of my catch. I was shocked to see it was a northern pike. It appeared to be slightly smaller than Tom's, but was a pike nonetheless, my first ever. As Tom scrambled for the net, the fish managed to shake the hook and just like that, the line went limp, and it was gone.

"I lost it!" I said in disbelief.

"Aw, dangit. That's too bad," Tom replied.

"Another northern!" Rob added.

I felt awful about not getting the fish in the boat. While the sport is in catching them, half of the fun is showing it off afterward. We fishermen are a needy group. Numbers, size, and species define our level of prowess. This need to impress explains our propensity for exaggeration and sometimes bold-faced lies. Our delicate pride is an unbecoming quality.

Eventually, Rob landed a small northern of his own. Pike of this size are called "hammer handles," as that is what they resemble, and about all that they are good for. Rob beamed with pride as Tom took it off the hook.

"Can we keep it?" Rob asked.

"Well, it is kind of small, but I suppose so," Tom replied.

"My first northern," Rob said. Of course, I was quickly reminded of my own first northern, still swimming freely somewhere below us.

With a catch to each of our credits, Tom thought it was time to head in for the day. He fired up the motor and we started back to the dock. When we tied up, we scrambled out of the boat, eager to tell Mom about our catches. Tom carried the stringer of the two pike up to the cabin and held it up.

"The little one is mine," Rob declared.

"Yeah, we all got one. Jimmy's got away, but he had a nice one too," Tom said.

"Wow! Well, let's get a picture of those. Go stand over by the trees and I'll take a snapshot," Mom said.

We walked over to a clearing with a backdrop of towering pines. Tom took off the big northern and said, "Jim, why don't you hold my fish since yours was almost as big."

"Are you sure?" I said. His offer seemed incredibly selfless. Like any good fisherman, Tom knew how I felt about losing one. I thought his idea for a photo with his fish was about the coolest thing ever. It was a lesson for Rob and me in humility, sportsmanship, and class.

"Yep. Here you go." He handed me the scale with the northern dangling by the lip. The finny beast was heavy in my seven-year-old hands. It was my substitute trophy for the one that got away. Next, Tom handed Rob his small northern and showed him how to hold it. Mom snapped a picture that captured the moment forever. Two brothers standing side by side strangely decked out in button-up dress shirts, showing off their catch. It was our proudest moment and one that set the stage for a future of unforgettable moments at the lake.

Forest Lake

The meaning of life?
Silly question for a boy
in a boat fishing.

Mom stopped dating Steve shortly after we went to the cabin in 1969. As it turned out, love and attraction could not be forced or faked, even when it came with a money clip. In the early seventies, she started dating Jack McKasy, a divorcee whose ex-wife and eight kids lived a couple blocks away from us on Portland Avenue. Jack seemed a better match for Mom than Steve. He was certainly more personable, down to earth and approachable. Occasionally on Saturdays, he and Mom took a selected few of each of their kids on picnic trips to beaches like Bayport or Lake Owasso. These were glorious outings filled with Frisbee, fishing, swimming and grilling out. Mom and Jack saw how much we liked to swim and horse around with the McKasy kids. Eventually they started taking us all camping together for long weekends at state parks. Little did any of us know years later we would become step-siblings when Mom and Jack married.

A few years into their dating, they decided to take some of us up to a cabin in Forest Lake. It was the beginning of a regular attempt to get us to a lake resort every year. I think Mom knew the importance of making everlasting memories for the family by putting us in an outdoor recreational setting for a week every year. At the end of the day, nothing was more important to her than family. These vacations—outings that often meant a lot of upfront work for her—were the key to that treasure chest of memories stored up in each of us over the years.

Forest Lake was less than an hour from our house in St. Paul, but to a kid, it felt like three. The resort as I remember it was small, five or six cabins stretched along a gravel driveway. It was run by a family that lived in a house at the top of the drive. The cabins were adequate in size for our large family at the time. They were no-frills affairs with multiple small bedrooms, a simplistic kitchen, and a living area with lots of well-worn but comfortable couches and chairs. Like most, they each had their own unique scent, musty like old books. The décor was basic, featuring curtains and bedspreads from another generation. These units had no fireplaces, so lacked the sooty, wood-smoke aroma so common in those further north, the best of all smells, perhaps.

There was also an old radio that worked if you treated it right. It required the touch of a safe cracker to tune in the closest rock and roll AM broadcast. Typically, we had to settle for a static-interrupted transmission that only got worse if someone turned on any other appliances. The television was an even bigger crapshoot. They were usually small, dated, and difficult to tune in to anything worth your time. Mom made it clear the cabin was not about watching TV. "We came here to get away from things like the TV," she'd remind everyone. The cabin was intended to be more about card games, jigsaw puzzles, and lots of outdoor time.

At the lake, none of us kids had much time for television, anyway. Instead, we relied on each other and the McKasy kids to entertain ourselves. Between all of us, someone was always finding something worth doing that was more fun than a fuzzy television screen. My sisters were always about lounge chairs, working on their tans and reading a good book. Of course, the allure of the beach meant plenty of time in the water for all of us kids on the hot days.

One of my favorite pastimes was throwing the football with Jack's son, Timmy. He was a couple years older than me and, being athletic and in our early teens, life pretty much revolved around ball sports. I was at an age where I lived and breathed football, due in large part to my worship of all things related to the Minnesota Vikings, perennial kings of the Central Division in those years. So, these chances to toss the pigskin around with Timmy was a great outlet for my teenage energy. Neither of us knew it at the time, but we would eventually become stepbrothers, so those days of hanging out at the cabin and on various camping trips set the stage for us brothers from other mothers.

* * *

My obsession with football led to idolizing my sister Patty's boyfriend, Patrick. He played for the Minnesota Gophers, and was a gentle giant, tall and muscular with a mellow demeanor. He dated Patty for a time in high school and his first year of college. She helped him keep up with his academic studies during the rigors of football practices and games over the course of the season. He was always extremely gracious to me. This was undoubtedly due to my sister telling him that I was a football junkie and that I played on the grade school team. Patrick probably had no idea how much I worshiped him as a gangly kid trying to make my own mark on the gridiron.

Patrick came up to Forest Lake and visited my sister for a day in 1974. The resort permitted guest visits and my sister saw the potential of him coming up as a possible chance to escape from what she saw as too much family time. It seems high school seniors weren't quite as into the family cabin experience as the rest of us. So, he visited for a day to give Patty a little relief.

There was a carnival in downtown Forest Lake that weekend and the two of them decided they would check it out. Knowing how much I looked up to Patrick, Patty invited me along. She'd always treated me decently as a kid, I think because I was the quiet one in the family. Because of our age difference, she and I didn't have many one-on-one experiences together, but those we shared remain fond memories for me. Being the eldest girl, she certainly had her moments as the raging Queen Bee of the family. Needless to say, I was glad to see her softer side come through and was grateful she felt compelled to invite me along.

Patrick drove us there in his old station wagon. We parked, got out and strolled around the carnival. This was one of those small, local affairs that traveled the state from town to town. The amusement rides creaked and hissed and groaned. They whipped and swirled brave patrons about in the name of providing a three-minute cheap thrill outside the riders' otherwise safe, mundane existence. The corn dog stands emanated their heavenly aroma, a mix of grease, batter and meat, a scent from the rougher side of heaven. The mouth-watering aromas combined with the flashing lights, game barkers, and the frenzy of all America's excesses in a single location, made it almost too much to take in. A delightful hammering of the senses.

We eventually came upon a game where qualifying for a prize meant throwing a football through a tire hanging fifteen feet away. *1 in wins a prize*, the slogan promised. I paused momentarily, mesmerized by the seemingly horrible business model of such an apparently simple game. The tire looked ridiculously close to the counter, despite having a hole smaller than any car rim could ever accommodate. These targets looked custom-made with the corrupt intent of ratcheting up the profit margin for carnival grifters wearing aprons full of other peoples' money. Despite the sketchy looking tire, I still wondered how the vendor could possibly come out ahead in such an easy transaction?

I remember thinking, I can do this.

"You want to give it a try, Jimmy?" Patrick asked.

I looked at him in disbelief. He must have sensed my interest. As a ninety-five pound, second-stringer on the eighth-grade team, I never had great confidence in myself. To have somebody believe in me and trust that I could meet a challenge meant a lot. Frankly, it caught me a bit off guard.

"C'mon, Jimbo, you can do it!" my sister said.

Knowing my sister was cheering me on upped the ante.

"Sure, I'll try."

Patrick paid a dollar to the game attendant who handed me the first of the footballs. On one side of me stood my idol, Patrick, next to him was Patty. The carnie stood behind the counter looking on, clearly the only one rooting against me. I was crushed by the audience of pressure but determined to show my passing prowess. I'd quarterbacked enough in my neighborhood sandlot games to know the mechanics of a decent spiral.

I gripped the ball at the laces, drew back and threw a dart right through the tire. My sister cheered, "Way to go, Jimbo!"

Patrick, who was always cool and subdued, responded, "Nice, Jimmy."

I took a deep breath and relaxed knowing I'd achieved the minimum to win a prize, and, more importantly, had proven myself to Patrick. Throws two and three, if successful, only meant a bigger prize.

My confidence was soaring as I took the second ball from the vendor. I pumped my arm and flung the pigskin toward the tire. It hit the rim and fell to the ground. I was dejected, but still riding the success of my first throw. The third attempt fell flat like the previous and was probably more indicative of the average person's experience, as well as my own true skill level. But still, one for three ain't bad.

I looked at the two Pats and shrugged my shoulders apologetically.

"It's okay, Jimbo. You still won!" my sister said.

"Yes, sir. Anything you want on the bottom shelf, kid." the carnie said, pointing to a row of ridiculously small stuffed animals. One thing was certain; they'd been purchased by the carnival operator for significantly less than $1.00 each.

I pointed to the Snoopy dog. The attendant plucked it from the shelf and handed it to me. I played it cool, like it was no big deal, but it really was. I'd never had any luck playing games at the Minnesota State Fair over the years, so this was a first. Even more importantly, I'd proven my skill to a guy I looked up to in both stature, and as an athlete. And, while it might seem a trivial victory for anyone else, it was a significant moment for me, a boy in his early teen years. It provided a boost in ego and self-confidence for the low, low price of one dollar.

* * *

That year in 1974 we happened to be at the cabin over the Fourth of July. With a family of four boys, one of us always seemed to find a way to get some fireworks for the occasion. Back then, they were much harder to get, more of a black-market item that had come from someone who had been to South Dakota and purchased some. On the night of the Fourth, we tried our best to keep all our fingers intact while igniting firecrackers, lady fingers, smoke bombs, and sparklers around camp. Cabin life sometimes affords opportunities for a level of lawlessness.

At dusk, we all gathered on blankets and lawn chairs and got ready to watch fireworks lakeside. We sprayed each other with clouds of bug repellent to ward off the thirsty, parasitic mosquitoes. Most of the other families gathered on blankets of their own. When the opening report went off with a thunderous boom over the water, the ooohhhs, and aaahhhs began from the crowd. The collective ooohhh'ing and aaahhh'ing became a group thing at nearly every starburst, but then tapered off to just the spectacular ones. It was a display like every small-town fireworks show ever, and over in twenty-five minutes. When it ended, we all filed back into our respective cabins, glad to be away from the voracious bugs.

The next morning, I decided to go out fishing alone. Each cabin was assigned a rowboat as part of their rental, so I grabbed a life preserver, tackle box, worms and my fishing rod and headed toward our boat.

Now, I'm not sure I ever got permission from Mom to take the boat out. I think the rule for us boys for the week was, if you're going out on the water, wear a life jacket. It seemed like a liberal policy given there were three of us, but it was a different time, and being at the cabin meant Mom could relax the rules a bit, as well.

I climbed in and situated myself between the oars. I untied the tether ropes from the dock and pushed off. My spindly arms pulled hard on the big, unwieldy oars in a rhythmic fashion with an occasional extra pull from the weaker left arm. It felt equal parts adventurous and freeing. I didn't know much about my father, but I knew he loved fishing and all things outdoors. Here I was rowing in his wake in search of a big fish.

I found a spot ten minutes up the shoreline from our cabin and dropped anchor. Forest Lake is densely populated with lake homes, all of them pushing piers out into the lake. These served as navigational reference points for my young, maritime skillset. I didn't want to get lost so made note of my location relative to the resort. Once I was oriented and anchored, I released the hook from the cork handle of my rod and baited it. Fat nightcrawlers were the bait of the day. I was out for bluegills or, maybe if I was lucky, some nice crappies.

I cast my line out and the waiting started. My brothers and I all grew up fishing, trained and tutored by the oldest, Tom. He'd learned his appreciation of the outdoor sports from our father before his violent death in 1967 (Dad was killed in a bar by a gang of men in a racially motivated incident). We'd learned from Tom that fishing is 95% patience. The other 5% was chaotic excitement when you fought and, with a bit of luck, landed an actual fish. With percentages like that, the math always computes in favor of those with lots of patience.

But, for myself, fishing has always been about more than just catching fish. I tend to gravitate to quiet places, places of self-isolation and peace. It is there I can reflect, regroup, and recharge. Fishing provides this refuge. In the woods and water, I am reminded how the human and natural systems are interconnected. I breathe easier, my heart rate drops, and a calmness overtakes me. It is better than any drug or stimulant that much is sure.

So, as I sat there waiting for my bobber to do its thing, I had lots of time to watch the fireworks debris float by in the form of paper and sticks, charred by their spent gunpowder rockets. Some were large enough to be part of the fireworks show I'd witnessed the night before. Most though, were of the household variety. Bottle rockets, firecracker paper, spent Roman candles, and other various whizzers and poppers.

Having grown up with an ecological awareness, seeing all the detritus from a single night's celebration floating around the boat caused me some sadness. What gave us rights as humans to trash up the lake to this level, all in the name of a single night's visual gratification? It was even more ironic that the cause of all of it was a celebration of our country's independence. I felt a little guilty for the role I had played in all of it. I pledged to be a better steward of the water in the future.

After an hour of casting and waiting, my bobber dove under the water with such force I knew it wasn't a bluegill toying with it, as so often happened. This was clearly different.

I reared back and set the hook as my brother taught me years earlier. The fight was on! I reeled my Zebco 101 with fury, letting up when the pull was heavy so as to not break the line. I had no leader and knew the sharp teeth of a northern pike could easily cut a line and leave me frustrated and cursing. I could tell by the way this fish fought and resisted; it was different.

After a minute or two I had the fish boatside. It was a thick, healthy seventeen-inch largemouth bass. I'd caught a bass before, but never anything nearly this big. The fish was intimidating. I wasn't even sure how to get it into the boat without breaking my line. I had no net.

I panicked and thought I'd row the boat back to the dock and deal with it on shore. I gave the fish enough line and positioned the rod such that I could tend it if needed. I hoisted the anchor and rowed with fury and purpose toward home.

I pulled up to the dock and secured the boat to it. I unhooked the fish, strung it, tied it to the dock, and raced to the cabin.

"Mom, I caught a huge bass!"

"Really? Where did you catch it?"

"I was out in the boat. Can you take a picture for me?"

"Sure. Let me grab the camera. Hold on."

Mom left and returned with our Kodak Instamatic. We walked back to the dock, and I pulled the fish out of the water.

"Wow, that *is* a nice one, Jimmy," Mom said.

I walked out to the middle of the dock dressed in my Saint Luke's football jersey and held the big bass up while Mom took a snapshot. I don't know why I've remembered this fish over the years. I've caught thousands over my life-time, so there had to be a reason this one stood out. I think it may have to do with the fact that I was alone in a boat at such a young age when I caught it. There is a certain pride which comes with catching such a lunker totally on one's own. Being the biggest fish I'd caught to that point in my life was enough to make it memorable. It certainly sealed my love for cabin life and all the adventure and excitement that comes along with a week up north. Even if up north was just forty-five minutes away.

16

Cedar Lake

Inside the torn screen
fluttering toward a small hole
a moth finds freedom.

In the late '70s, after a couple years of calling Forest Lake our cabin, Mom decided to upgrade to a place farther away. There's something to be said for getting *way* away, and Forest Lake just wasn't it. A little too close to the Twin Cities. Her search led to reserving a cabin on Cedar Lake near Aitkin, Minnesota, about a two-and-a-half-hour drive from our house in St. Paul.

The resort consisted of about eight cabins sprinkled along a long, gently sloped gravel driveway that traversed the property. Over the years we stayed in a few different units at Morningside, all humble with the requisite old furniture, hodge-podge collection of dishes, and suffering from substandard water pressure. At the time we just sort of rolled with some of the inconveniences of the place, in part because we didn't know any better. Besides, much of the whole cabin experience was held in the charm of old furniture and just a bit of inconvenience. If you didn't want that, you should probably just stay home. Looking back on our history of cabins though, Morningside was probably the resort that was the least well-maintained.

While Morningside held all the promise of fishing and swimming in beautiful Cedar Lake, one of the more alluring attractions for me as a teenager was the resort owner's daughter, Liz. She was an attractive blonde with a stunning figure for her young age. The problem was, she knew she was good looking and used it as needed. Beauty was her weapon of choice. She was flirty with all the camp boys, including my brothers and me. She pranced around working her assigned chores, taking notice of which teenage boys were in the area at any given time.

It is funny how these week-long resort romances and flirtations develop, grow, and eventually fizzle out by the Saturday checkout time. I'd always held secret crushes on my twin stepsisters at the Forest Lake cabin, so these battles with cabin-induced romance were nothing new to me. As teens, we were all hormonally raging anyway. When mixed with the great outdoors and the freedom to roam about camp, it was just the right recipe for puppy love.

It wasn't a one-way street with the flirtations either. As an adolescent on the make, I couldn't help but notice where Liz was at any given moment during the long days at Morningside. Accordingly, I was strategic about placing myself in her sphere whenever possible. The cat-and-mouse games went on for a few days early in the week. By Wednesday or so, me and every other teenage male had seen enough of Liz's drama and pouting to know her personality would simply be too much work. It was all high drama from the drama queen.

* * *

As circumstances would have it, another cabin crush developed one year when I was in high school. A farm family came up from Iowa for a week at Morningside. In a resort setting, it is easy to see the license plates on the cars of your neighbors and discover where people are from. There were always plenty of Minnesota plates, but usually some from Wisconsin, Illinois and Iowa as well. Minnesota's vast number of lakes was an attraction for the entire upper Midwest region.

If the license plate didn't give this family away, the father sure did. He had the whole Iowa agricultural package. A farmer's tan accompanied by pale white chicken-skin legs that hadn't seen the sun since he was knee high to the corn he grew. All of this was topped off by a seed cap worn for most of the week. His presence screamed, "I'm from Iowa, here on vacation!" None of this is to say they were bad people, just an observation from a self-proclaimed, sophisticated Minnesota city boy.

They were a family of four; mother, father, and two kids. I couldn't help but take immediate notice of their daughter, an impossibly cute blonde girl aptly named, Bonita. I was at the age where I could spot a good-looking girl from four hundred yards, but still had trouble seeing that the dishwasher needed to be unloaded. I was a teenager with a firm grasp on my selective vision.

As the week went on, a gang of us kids in the same age group slowly started hanging out more and more. Bonita occupied my brain most of the time, whether I was with her or not. We'd exchanged glances on occasion across the circle of friends, but I was trying to play it cool. Not knowing how to do this cat-and-mouse game of love, I assumed cool and aloof was what would attract someone as stunning as Bonita. I was also exceedingly shy with most people, especially girls. I just didn't know how to conduct myself.

One night late in the week, the gang was out and about as I sat in my cabin eating popcorn and reading a book. Books and seclusion just seemed easier than all that went into socializing with friends. Apparently at some point in the evening, Bonita inquired as to where I was, and my brothers brought her and a couple other kids to our cabin.

"Hey Jim, we're going to go by the beach and play some games, wanna come with?" my brother Rob asked.

I sat there nervously eating popcorn, struggling with the decision of spending time with Bonita and the gang, or just being alone. My struggle was real.

"I dunno. I think I'll just stay in tonight and read," I said.

"C'mon, Jim, don't be a pooper," Liz said.

I popped more kernels in my mouth, deliberating on the pros and cons of each scenario. I hated my shyness and all it denied me in life. Why couldn't I be social like the rest of the kids? Was there something inherently wrong with me? Was I weird?

"Nah, I think I'll just hang out here," I replied.

Bonita appeared to be a little dejected that I was not willing to run with the pack. I wanted to scream, "It's not you, it's me!" By the end of the week, Bonita was my complete and total obsession. I'd even worked up my plan for our inevitable departure. I schemed that on their way out on Saturday, I would offer to exchange addresses with her so we could write to each other and continue our relationship, or at least the relationship I had in my head. We'd really had no grounds for anything, other than a lot of flirtatious glances over the course of the week. For me though, that was enough to justify the start of a long-distance pen pal gig that would no-doubt lead to marriage and a gaggle of kids in some small town in Iowa.

Of course, when the time came to leave on Saturday, I couldn't muster up the courage to approach Bonita and make the offer. Instead, I stood there dumbly, waving as her family's car pulled out the drive back to the highway. My shyness and I were alone again, left to figure out how love and courtship work on another day. These vacation puppy love affairs were almost too much for a sixteen-year-old to bear. The cabin life was a whole lot easier when all that mattered was how many fish you caught. Women made everything more complex!

* * *

Like most cabin vacations, time at Morningside was spent between hanging out on the beach, swimming, fishing out in the boat, and lots of grilled food. One of my favorite activities though, was the occasional pickup game of volleyball. These were rag-tag gatherings, everything from seven-year-old kids to out-of-shape, pot-bellied dads. I always loved the sport itself and was finally of a stature that I could spike with abandon and was happiest playing the net. I was over six feet tall with long, gangly arms but not afraid to hit the ground and dig an epic save.

The matches were long, drawn-out affairs with each side picking up players as the game wore on. Shouts, laughter, and raucous chiding usually attracted people from other cabins. Matches often started with four players on a team and gradually built up to ten or twelve on a side. Having that many players on a team made for some spectacularly long volleys. Furthermore, the games served to bring the resort together. Families and cabins of strangers came to the court and helped each other keep a ball in the air.

During play, there was passing and setting between kids and adults alike, with plenty of apologies for gaffs and compliments for heroic saves. Considering the casual nature of camp, there were plenty of illegal hits as well; open-palmed, two-handed slaps mixed in with overhead carries. At this skill level the only rule truly enforced was three hits per side. People were a whole lot more relaxed on vacation than those on the gym floor at the YMCA. It seemed at Morningside, volleyball was the great unifier and equalizer. It certainly made my own camp experience more enjoyable.

* * *

Late in the week of our stay at Morningside, the adults started to get restless. They loved the fact that being at the lake brought everyone together, but like any parents they needed some adult time. I meant a chance to get away from the multitudes of kids that roamed from cabin-to-cabin foraging for snacks and pop. So, Mom, Jack and my sister Patty usually reserved one night during the week where they went into Aitkin to get dinner and some cocktails at a supper club. Patty was of legal age and tagged along because she'd had enough of us kids for the week. We teens knew the parents would be out late and, frankly, the thought of less oversight for an evening sounded okay to us anyway. Ground rules were set by Mom before they left and some-times even adhered to.

On these nights, we ran feral until dusk when the mosqui-toes drove us into our cabins. Once inside, we played cards, board games, and listened to the local rock station. This station always played a music selection radically different from what we heard back in the cities. While the songs were all familiar—Top 40 radio—the playlist was usually more eclectic. Because they were the only rock station around, they had to satisfy a broader audience. The result was a confus-ing mix ranging from Barry Manilow to Bachman Turner

Overdrive, Air Supply to Zeppelin. The stark transition between the styles was both refreshing and annoying. The fact that there was no other option meant that you had to suffer through a song you deplored to get to one you loved. Like many other minor annoyances at the cabin, this was part of the experience that made it memorable.

We popped popcorn, worked on jigsaw puzzles, or read old magazines from the bookshelves. When we got tired of indoor activities, we went outside and played hide-and-seek or hung out on the dock. Out on the water we gazed at the heavens, a tapestry of stars and planets not visible in the light-polluted skies back in the cities. It was a reminder of our smallness in the universe as well as the natural beauty uncovered by life at the cabin, one not possible back home.

Sometime well after 11:00 on one of these adult nights, my mom, Jack, and Patty came home. My brothers were asleep, and I was laying on the couch reading when they walked in. Judging from their boisterousness, they'd been drinking. I sat up on the couch only to see there was a fourth person with them. He was a big, muscular guy with a mustache and an apparent romantic interest in my sister.

Mom was clearly a few drinks in when she introduced me.

"Jimmy, do you know who this is?" she asked.

I looked at the guy and he didn't strike me as someone I knew. I shrugged.

"Would you believe it if I said he was one of the Purple People Eaters?" she asked. Her reference was to the name given to the legendary defensive line of the Minnesota Vikings during the '70s.

Given that clue, I pegged him right away. "Is this Gary Larsen?" I responded in disbelief.

"It most certainly is," Mom replied. "We met him at the restaurant, and I told him I have a son who worshiped him and the rest of the Purple Gang."

Mom's introduction put Gary and me in an awkward position. It's true the Viking great was a hero of mine, but I'm sure the adulation of a sixteen-year-old kid was down his list for memorable ways to spend a weeknight in Aitkin, Minnesota. I said hello and shook his big, meaty hand. I was in the midst of greatness, but I tried to play it cool and downplay my fawning as I knew celebrities probably hated that sort of thing. In my own head I was kneeling before him saying "I'm not worthy!" Jack headed to the kitchen to make everyone a drink, so after a couple of more awkward minutes, I said I was going to go to bed.

"Nice meeting you," I said.

"You too," he replied.

I went to my room, dressed in my pajamas, and crawled into bed. I lay there conflicted. It was a strange combination of being star-struck and yet wanting to protect my sister from his advances, if that was what he was looking to do. Or maybe she was trying to encourage it? I wasn't sure. At the same time, I was pretty sure my sister was happy I was out of the picture altogether. Who needs a kid brother chaperone? But accompanying my protective thoughts were my celebrity regrets. I should have asked him for his autograph. Maybe even asked for a picture with him. Why didn't I do that? Sometimes in the presence of distinction, one's mind just goes blank.

I have no idea what happened after I fell asleep. He was gone in the morning. I don't recall asking Pat, Mom, or Jack anything specific either. Mom just said they met him at the supper club. It seemed she was as star-struck as me over the whole encounter, maybe even more so. Mom was as loyal and intense a fan as I was, so she held him up high too.

I guess it was our family's three-hour brush with fame, as insignificant as it may have been. What are the chances you're going to run into an NFL star in a restaurant in the middle of nowhere in the middle of the week? I suppose it is one of the intangible, unexpected benefits of a night up at the cabin. One not easily forgotten.

*　*　*

We never had much success fishing on Cedar Lake. This isn't to say we didn't give it the old college try. We tried deep and shallow, shore to shore and never seemed to catch anything more than an occasional panfish. From a fishing standpoint, it was a great disappointment for us as a lake.

One year, my sister Jane's father in-law came up with his wife. Johnny and Myrtle were about the nicest couple I'd ever met. With years of happy marriage under their belts, along with a handful of grown kids, they still clearly loved each other. There was lots of delicate teasing between them, the kind of fake arguing that is a show of affection and a polite airing of differences. There was no bite to their gentle banter.

Johnny was a retired railroad man, who'd put in his best years working hard for the rail industry. One day at the cabin we heard a train whistle and Johnny said, "Take your hat off and put your hand over your heart, people." It was all in jest, but it showed his allegiance with a bit of humorous flair.

Johnny also loved to fish, so my brother Rob and I decided we'd take him out in the motorboat and try our luck. Johnny showed up to the dock in his wide-brimmed straw hat and all his gear. He was quite a sight with his stocky build and his bulbous nose. Johnny looked a bit like WC Fields with a fishing rod. Rob and I grabbed the nightcrawlers and our gear and loaded the boat. It was a rental, so by the time the three of us got situated, it was a little bit like rub-a-dub, three men in a tub, but we didn't care. We were going to have some fun even if it was powered by a nine-horsepower Johnson with its best years behind it.

I choked the engine, fired it up until it was warm, and we were off. We putted along on the calm lake to an area of lily pads that looked to hold some promise. I killed the motor and Rob dropped the anchor and we all began to cast our lines. Rob and I tried using artificial baits hoping to catch something of size and significance. Johnny was content to try for bluegills and crappies, maybe even enough for a fish dinner.

Rob and I cast with fury and intent. After a dozen casts we switched lures to find something more effective in our tackle boxes. Our efforts were only met with disappointment. After forty minutes, Johnny's bobber took a dive and he reeled in a four-inch-long bluegill, too small to keep. It was a bright spot, but only temporarily. After another half hour of futility, we moved to another spot across the lake, then a third. By then, Johnny's patience was waning, and his sense of humor took over.

"There ain't no fish in this lake, Jim," he said.

I had to laugh because I was beginning to think he was right. One measly catch among three guys is kind of pathetic. Like any good group of fishermen, it was easier to blame the lake than our angling savvy. Twenty action-free minutes later, he said it again. "Ain't no fish in this lake, Jim." It became his ongoing mantra as we moved, fished, and moved again.

After a couple hours of our lives lost under the hot summer sun, Johnny made a recommendation. "Well, gentlemen, maybe it's time we go in and recapitulate."

Playing off his use of a ten-dollar word, I said. "That sounds like it would hurt." Without missing a beat, he said, "Not if you put some salve on it."

I cracked up at his quick wit and hilarious comeback. Johnny's nature was cantankerous and wily. He was one who roared like a lion but was really a pussycat at heart.

As I fired up the Johnson for the ride in, it occurred to me that while our time fishing had been a bust, it had served a different purpose. Time in the boat gave me the chance to get to know Johnny, a distant relative, a little better. I'd gone into the boat a bit apprehensive about fishing with a guy I hadn't talked to much in the past. When all was said and done, I'd come out understanding we shared a sense of humor and wit. We'd bonded in a way we might not have, had we stayed ashore.

And I think there's a certain value in that. Time on the water, fishing, talking, and relaxing with others has a way of bringing everyone a little closer. Maybe this is a subconscious, ulterior motive the sport holds for me. Fishing is fun, but half of the fun is the banter in the boat. Sometimes the fish aren't biting but the words are, in tender, joking ways. One thing is sure, there's certainly been some keepers over the years.

* * *

In the summer of 1986, I was unemployed and having no luck finding work. I was laid off in May from my first post-college real job at a mapping firm in Minneapolis. I was devastated by the news that I, along with ten others, were being let go because of federal cutbacks under the Reagan administration. After the layoff I moved back in with my mom and shared a bedroom with my brother, Paul.

There is something demoralizing about losing your independence after living on your own for a time. The humiliation of losing a job and living with my mom put me in the closest thing to a depression I've ever encountered. I gained weight, spent my days job hunting, mountain biking, and generally feeling sorry for myself. It was not a good period in my life.

One bright spot that summer was looking forward to our trip to Morningside Resort. The cabin was always an escape from the woes of city life, so I looked at it as a chance to get away and try and relax a little.

That year I shared a cabin with Mom, my sister Jane, and her three kids under the age of four. Nicolas, my godson, was almost four, Stephanie was fifteen months, and Jennifer was three months. If that sounds like a cabin full, it was. I've always loved kids though, so this arrangement didn't really phase me when it was mentioned.

Jane's husband, Steve, worked road construction, so was unable to come up for the week. This left her with the three kids, but we figured with the support of Mom and me, she'd be able to handle it. And handle it she did. It was *me* who surprised everyone.

If you ask anyone who knows me, they will tell you I don't rattle easily. I am a stoic German/Swede, not gifted in emotional expression, to say the least. A straight-line grin on my face usually means I'm having a blast. In my angriest state I might wrinkle my brow or grit my teeth a little. I am an even-keel guy.

Anyway, the week started cool and rainy and stayed that way for most of the duration. During the breaks when the sun came out there was beach, paddle boat, and fishing time, but the large part of our days were spent indoors. Keeping the kids entertained became a full-time job. There were books, puzzles, and various toys, but being cooped up by an all-day rain begins to wear on kids and adults alike.

Because I was still single and self-absorbed, I had the boundaries and expectations of someone who's never had to deal with kids on a 24/7 schedule. As "Uncle Jim," I had the luxury of rent-a-kid, where I took one or more of the nieces or nephews to a park for some kite flying, or to the zoo, or out for ice cream, until such time as I'd had enough. Then, I could deliver them back to my sisters, fed, entertained, and happy, and go about my self-important life. Overall, I would say I was an engaged uncle, all things considered. But it was always on my terms. Those terms usually had a three-hour window to them. Then it was back to mom and dad!

On Wednesday of our week, after a long afternoon of kids in varying degrees of emotional happiness and distress, we sat down as a group to eat dinner. Mom set out the food and Jane took care of cutting it up for Nick and Steph and spoon-feeding Jennifer. Nick sat in a booster seat, Stephanie was relegated to a highchair and Jane sat with Jennifer on her lap. I was witnessing all the chaos and orchestration that goes into a family meal. Lots of prep just to feed and water a young family.

I was about to discover that any meal with three or more kids typically takes an hour to prepare, thirty minutes to clean up, and exactly seven minutes to eat before the whole thing breaks down in an emotional Hindenburg.

A few minutes into dinner, Stephanie let out a high-pitched scream that still echoes over Cedar Lake, I'm sure. I looked at her and then turned to my sister, wondering what just happened.

"Stephanie, no, no. Eat your food," Jane said calmly.

Stephanie looked at Jane and screamed again. Same pitch and an even greater volume. Again, I looked at her, then Jane.

"She does this lately, Jim. It's her latest thing," Jane said.

Even Mom looked a little surprised at the second defiant scream and tried to stifle a grin. Having raised seven of us, it was the type of behavior she'd likely seen out of one or more of us at some point. Most mothers have.

"Stephanie, no, no. No more, okay?" Jane said.

We all resumed our eating. After a couple minutes she screamed a third time. It absolutely rattled my fillings.

"Stephanie!" I shouted; my nerves frayed to breaking point. I glared at her as she showed surprise at her uncle's outburst.

Mom, Jane, and the rest of the table all looked at me in shock and surprise. Who was this guy? To be honest, I was a little surprised myself. My normally cool and calm demeanor had succumbed to the culmination of a day cooped up with three kids. From a single person's perspective, the whole week had been an argument for birth control.

Jane gave me a look of disbelief.

Mom jumped in as referee of the moment, "Now, Jim, she's not even two yet. You need to understand that."

Guilt rushed over me. I think I'd pissed off my sister for the first time since we were kids ourselves. I'd lost my cool in front of her whole family. Here she was, trying to single-parent her way through a rainy week at the cabin and her brother can't handle a little screaming at dinner? What did I expect when I signed up for this deal?

"Wait till you have kids, Jim," Jane said.

I felt horrible, but I'd been provoked by the sum-total of the day's events, and I'd let them get the better of me.

"Sorry. Long day," I replied.

We all went back to eating our dinner and, near as I can remember, the screaming subsided from thereon out.

The story has lived on over the years. My sisters Pat and Jane both had children years before us brothers did, so of course we boys were quick to offer unsolicited advice. Once, when one of Jane's kids was acting up, Rob said, "Jane, can't you control your kids?" Some words stand the test of time, and these were a good example.

Both my outburst at the cabin and Rob's comment to Jane were brought up when Rob and I were deep in the throes of parenting our own two-year-olds, years later. Jane used the quote on both Rob and me more than once in jest as our patience wore thin with our own kids during their temper tantrums. Her teases were entirely warranted and justified. Rob and I found out the hard way after moving on from the years of bachelorhood into parenting, that karma is a bitch.

* * *

Our years at Morningside were good years. They were pivotal in defining the importance of getting as much of the family as possible up to a resort for a week together. As we all grew up, married and started having kids, we began to rent additional cabins of our own at the resort just so we could continue the annual tradition of going up north. Our years there saw me to pass from my adolescent years to college and eventually into early marriage. Time together at the beach, in the boat, and around the dinner table brought forth the beauty and sometimes the struggles of our family. It was our chance to slow down and talk at a deeper level. In that respect, Morningside will always hold a special place in my heart. It was cabin life, defined.

Crooked Lake

*The light from the dock
the soft lapping of water
a writer could paint.*

When I was a freshman in college, my friend Pete invited me to his folks' cabin near Deerwood, Minnesota. They called the place the Timbers, and it was essentially a timeshare vacation home they split with two other families. The cabin was a short two-hour drive from the Twin Cities, a perfect distance for a frequent getaway. The one requirement tied to my invitation was that I help Pete with a little manual labor over the weekend. They were replacing some steps that wound from the cabin to the lake. The steps were comprised of short sections of railroad ties dug into the hillside. Being strong young men with good backs, we were enlisted as the cheap labor solution.

The Timbers was set back amongst a forest of tall pines that served as the inspiration for the name. It was a beautiful old structure with the traditional log and mortar construction that gives a good cabin that rustic, up-north feel immediately upon entering. Places like these were three-season dwellings, being much too drafty and poorly insulated to make residency bearable during the brutal Minnesota winters.

The interior was tasteful and spectacular. The knotty pine walls, simplistic electrical wiring and beautiful hardwood floors gave the place a comfortable, minimalist feel. An impressive fieldstone fireplace served as the focal point of the living room. Bedrooms were small but comfortable, and the whole place had that familiar cabin smell of wood smoke, throw rugs and old books.

There were a couple of moments that stood out during that weekend visit with Pete and his family. One of them was an evening game of canasta. I'd never played a card game that required essentially two decks of cards. It was great fun learning the game, especially at night on a screen porch in the middle of the Minnesota woods. Moments like these with popcorn and root beer simply could not be recreated in the noisy, chaotic surroundings that made up our urban lives back home.

The other eventful memory during my stay with the Graysons came the next afternoon. Pete's father asked if we wanted to go water skiing. I'd never done it before, but I was eager to give it a try. The thought of strapping two pieces of wood to my feet and being dragged behind a screaming forty-horsepower engine on a lake sounded both terrifying and exhilarating. I considered myself an athletically capable kid, so I figured strength and coordination wouldn't be the issue, as much as form and technique. I would never know unless I tried.

Pete's little brother, Jon, wanted to go too, so the four of us piled into the speedboat and took our seats. It was decided that because Pete had skied before, he would go first. As I saw it, I needed to learn what I could from him before my turn at the end of the water whip. I was a bit nervous and if any techniques or nuances of the sport could be picked up as a spectator, then I was all eyes.

Pete put on his life vest and jumped over the side.

"Throw him the rope, Jim," Mr. Grayson said.

I gathered up the rope and flung it out to Pete once his skis were secured. He paddled over to the line and grabbed the handle while Mr. Grayson positioned the boat and tightened the slack. When the line between us was taut, Pete shouted, "Hit it!"

Pete's dad slammed down the throttle and the bow of the boat lifted out of the water at the mercy of the motor's thrust. Pete's little brother Jon and I held on as the boat lurched ahead. After a few seconds of struggle and dragging, Pete was upright and behind us in the wake of our engine. He made the launch look easy. It gave me hope and calmed my anxiety a bit.

Pete was deft at the sport. He cut sharp turns in the calm areas outside the wake, throwing elegant arcs of water from his skis in a display of showmanship. When he crossed over the waves of the wake, he did it with skill and nonchalance. It was clear this wasn't his first rodeo. If I was looking for a skiing mentor, I needed to look no further.

Eventually he fatigued and let go of the tow rope. He slowed and sank as his dad circled around to fetch him. We pulled up alongside and he hoisted himself in with the help of a short ladder on the rear of the boat.

"Whew, that was fun!"

"You're a pretty good skier, Pete," I said.

"Thanks. Now it's your turn."

I was still fairly trepidatious about the speed and thoughts of falling badly, despite it being into the softness of a lake. Nevertheless, I nodded and cinched up my life jacket. My chance to cross this sport off my list of life experiences was upon me and I embraced the idea like hugging a creepy uncle.

I jumped in and waited as Pete pushed each of the skis across the water in my direction. I grabbed them and began the awkward process of stepping into the rubber bindings. I flailed and thrashed as I tried to keep my head above water, my feet in front of me and my anxiety at bay. I imagine from a fish's perspective I looked a lot like a man in the process of trying to drown himself. All of it was harder than Pete had made it look.

After I managed to get the skis on and conduct an infinite number of positional adjustments, I deemed myself as ready as I could be.

I shouted, "Hit it!"

The motor revved as I gripped the tow rope handle and held on. I surged forward, the whole time experiencing a firehose effect. My face was blasted with water funneled between my skis in some sort of aquatic nightmare starring fireman Satan himself. I began to wonder what appeal anyone saw in this version of recreational water boarding. After five seconds of near-drowning, I let go of the rope. I assumed I must have been doing something wrong, as nothing could be that torturous.

Mr. Grayson turned the boat around and came alongside me.

"I was back here eating water, Pete. Is that the way it's supposed to be?" I asked.

"Yeah, it kinda is for the first few yards. You just have to tough it out until you pop out of the water."

"Okay, then. Just checking."

So, evidently, I wasn't doing it wrong, but rather the nasal-clearing start was part of the fun. I hoped the second part was more fun than the first.

I regrouped, grabbed the tow rope and positioned myself again.

"Okay, hit it!"

This time I got further than the first, but my ski tips dipped under water and suddenly my legs were behind me and I was being pulled headlong through the water. *I am Aquaman!* Knowing this impossibly bad form was not going to correct itself, I let go of the rope again.

The third time was not much better. It seemed the force of the boat and the drag of the skis bent my body in the shape of the letter 'C'. I was a human drag chute, a hundred-and-fifty-pound anchor at the end of a long rope. The whole exercise seemed absurd, but I was determined to get upright and prove myself.

I made a couple more attempts, each time progressing a little further before splashing back down. After the fifth time or so, I heard Pete's brother Jon say, "Dad, he's using up all our gas. There won't be enough for my turn."

I felt bad, but his statement must have fueled something in me because on the next try I popped out of the water and suddenly was upright in the safety of the boat's wake. My skis slapped and skittered on top of the bubbling water, still churning from the propeller. Once I was up, the whole task was significantly easier. It was simply a matter of balancing and holding on for dear life.

As we sped around the lake at mid-throttle, I quickly realized the appeal of the sport. It was both as terrifying and exhilarating as I had expected. Here I was like the disciple Peter on top of the water wondering if my faith was strong enough to keep me here. I was actually water skiing for the first time, and it felt miraculous! The wind in my hair, the whine of the motor and the strain of my arms as I clung to the rope of life were all part of an amazing ride. I'd struggled like any beginner, but in the end, I'd prevailed.

After about five minutes, my confidence exceeded my focus and I crashed ungracefully in a pile of limbs, skis and splash. The initial impact took my breath away, especially because it was so abrupt and unexpected. Once the crash was over, I realized I was floating in the softness of the lake water, having gone from 30 miles an hour to zero in the span of a few feet. I was a water-borne crash test dummy, and my fall was a complete rush!

Mr. Grayson pulled the boat alongside and congratulated me on my first successful ride.

"Nice job! Do you want to go again?"

"No, thanks. I think I'm good for now. It was a blast, though!"

I was feeling accomplished and didn't want to tempt fate and perhaps fail again. I'd proven I could do it, and for now, that was good enough. Learning this new sport was an exercise in determination. I've always struggled with my self-confidence, having an inner critic that never lets up. Moments like this day gliding on top of Crooked Lake helped me quiet the beast, at least temporarily. It was a notch in my list of accomplishments that, as insignificant as it was, helped me to believe in myself just a little more. And as a teenager, those self-esteem building moments are as important as anything else in life.

* * *

A couple years later, Pete invited a whole gang of our college friends up to the Timbers for a weekend stay in the fall. Of course, as college kids, "weekend stay" translates to a party, so that's more along the lines of what it was. The agenda was beer, music, games, and fun. We all lived within five miles of each other, so a trip to the woods for some down-time sounded like a great idea. I offered to bring up my stereo to provide the musical entertainment. I was a music nut and, like many kids my age, had a kicking stereo with tall, powerful speakers.

At the time, a few of us were dating others in our little clique of friends. I was dating Carol at the time. She was an attractive young blonde woman of many talents. She was a gifted photographer, an adept guitarist, and had a good eye for art and craftsmanship. Carol also rode a Honda 360 motorcycle giving her broad personality an even wider arc. We were fairly compatible and had been dating a while. She was my first real girlfriend, and I was still trying to navigate the intricacies of what it meant to be in a relationship.

Besides the two of us, there was Pete and his girlfriend Amy, our friends Doug and Pat, as well as Ellen, Beth, Mary Jo, Rosie and her boyfriend. It was a houseful. We were a tightly-knit group and frequently went dancing to bands like Raggs, Chameleon, and Home Free at local clubs in the Twin Cities. We also played together on some college intramural teams, went to concerts, and attended the same universities. As a group we just enjoyed the company of one another during those collegiate years. As I noted, a few romances served as the core of the group, but for the most part we were just traveling down the same track at this point in our lives, happy to have the others aboard.

When we arrived at the Timbers, we all investigated the bedroom situation. The women claimed the carriage house above a small garage, while the guys split between the cabin and the boat house. Ultimately, we would all share time together in the main cabin, but the number of beds and distributed nature of the buildings made it necessary to split up the sleeping accommodations.

As evening set in, the beer started flowing. I set up the stereo and kept it thumping with albums from Bob Seger, Bruce Springsteen, and The Cars. I was obsessed with all of them and had an impressive album and cassette tape library to show for it. Had I known then what I know now, I would have left the stereo back home and enjoyed the quiet of the Northwoods. But, being college kids, it was all about noisy parties.

That night the festivities floated between the cabin and the boathouse. People came and went, and I was really digging it all. There was something about having no supervising adults amongst us that flipped a switch in everyone. We had the run of the place, and between the chaos of a beer buzz, the blasting music, and lots of goofing around, it was all so bohemian.

I managed to get so caught up in myself and the spontaneity of everything, that I lost track of Carol. Realizing I hadn't seen her in a while I started looking around for her. Eventually, I caught up with Amy and asked, "Hey, have you seen Carol around?"

"Actually, Jim, she's up in the carriage house crying right now," she said.

"What? Crying? Why?" I asked, clueless.

"She feels like you're ignoring her. She's pretty upset."

I was devastated. In my obsession with my own fun—socializing and forever futzing with the damn stereo—it became clear I had neglected a key person in my life. How stupid could a guy be?

"Aw, crap. I feel horrible. Could you do me a favor and tell her how sorry I am and that I want to talk it out?"

"I'll do what I can, but no promises. As I said, she is pretty upset."

I returned to the party feeling like the fool I was. Nothing makes me feel worse than letting someone down. The party was suddenly becoming just a little less party for me.

A short while later, we found our way back to each other. Carol seemed reserved and sad. I walked up to her and said, "Hey, do you want to take a walk to the boathouse so we can talk?"

"Sure."

We strolled down the dirt path to the boathouse. The music and echoes of the party we'd left thumped and swirled behind us as we walked hand in hand. Thankfully the boathouse was empty when we walked in. We moved over to a small couch where we sat and talked.

"I'm sorry I neglected you tonight. I guess I just got caught up in everything," I said.

"I felt ignored. Every time I thought we were going to hang out and be with one another, you got up to change the music or something."

"I guess I didn't even realize that."

"It's just, us girls like attention once in a while, ya know?"

"I get it. I will definitely try and work on that."

I leaned into her, and we kissed hard and long, happy to be together again after our brief separation. As we kissed, things heated up. We were ten minutes into groping when we heard someone coming down the path. The door handle jiggled and we quickly recombobulated and tried to make it look like we were just sitting and talking. In walked Doug, who seemed to sense what he'd interrupted. We exchanged awkward hellos as he continued through out to the dock.

Carol and I looked at each other and busted out laughing. Our little make-out session was clearly over. Our fiery encounter had been doused by Doug's cameo appearance and that was that.

"Should we head back up to the party?" I asked.

"Yeah."

"I'm glad we talked," I said. I was relieved we had patched things up and grateful it wouldn't hang over us the whole weekend. I am both a pacifist and non-confrontational, so this kind of ripple in a relationship with anyone made me almost physically ill.

As we held hands and walked back to the main cabin, I thought about the emotional ups and downs I'd experienced in the span of the last two hours. When I'd heard Carol had been in tears, I was almost brought to them myself. That was followed by the joy and elation of making up and out. I was learning that dating was a dance that takes work, and along with the graceful twirls and dips come moments of stepping on each other's toes.

This was my first real exposure to some of the heartbreak and difficulties that come along in a relationship. People want acknowledgment. Relationships are a movement away from individualism and toward the betterment of the body of "us." At the Timbers, I was still mired in the selfishness that was part-and-parcel of my twenties. Carol was my first real girlfriend and was unwittingly steering me in the direction of how to properly treat someone with affection. And while I will always remember it as a wild, fun weekend, this revelation was still the biggest take-away from it.

* * *

The festivities at the Timbers ebbed and flowed over the course of the weekend. There were board games, cards, and lots of beer and laughter. Dan had brought his boat up, so there were a few boat rides as well. We were college kids pretending like we owned the place and blowing off a little steam away from the rigors of our studies. It felt good to be in the woods with my friends.

On Sunday, people woke up and started packing for the trip home. Pat, Dan, and I were in the kitchen looking to get some breakfast. I poured a bowl of Captain Crunch and milk.

"I'm going to have the Jim Morrison special," Pat said.

He grabbed a beer from the refrigerator and popped it open. He poured it on top of his Captain Crunch as a few of the women strolled in.

Pat was often the life of the party. His sense of humor was blistering, and he lived to laugh and make others do the same. His antics and spontaneity made him unpredictable and erratic as we were witnessing with his barley-and-hop-soaked breakfast. Pat was big into The Doors, especially the wild and tragically sad life of Jim Morrison. His cereal joke paid homage to the line from "Roadhouse Blues" that goes, "Well, I woke up this morning, I got myself a beer." Pat always loved that line and took it to the next level by pouring the beer on his cereal.

Most of the gang stood and laughed in disbelief at Pat as he munched his sugary suds. After a couple of minutes, they strolled away in disbelief to resume their packing. Pat looked up at Dan and I and said, "That's enough of this. Funny is funny, but that's just gross." He dumped the rest of the bowl into the garbage.

Laughing, he said, "I had to try it. If for nothing else than for shock value."

"Yeah, Morrison would be proud," I replied.

It was a classic Pat moment. He was always quick to get a laugh, often by doing something outside the conventional lines. At the same time, the incident was indicative of the truth of who we really were versus who we worshiped and aspired to emulate. He and I always looked to rock stars as cool dudes that had it easy with drugs, sex, and rock and roll. We both knew that persona didn't hold water for us and wasn't truly our nature anyway. We were way safer and more conservative than any Hollywood rock star BS. But none of that meant we couldn't have some fun with faking it at times. The weekend at the Timbers was about as close as we came to that fast-lane lifestyle. And when the dust had all settled, the only thing that mattered was hanging out with good friends in a pristine setting on Crooked Lake.

Pleasant Lake

Swimming between docks
the boy searches the bottom
for sunken treasures.

In the late '90s, Mom started looking into changing up our cabin situation. While our years at Morningside Resort were good ones, Mom's standards had risen. The Morningside owners didn't appear as invested in the place as they once were. The cabins weren't as clean or as well-maintained as when we'd first started staying there. When Mom mentioned it to the owners, her gripes were met with indifference. Knowing there were plenty of other options, her mind was set on trying somewhere new. Her main requirement was to be on a lake, with clean, modern cabins. But most of all, it needed to have enough units so everyone from the family who wanted one, had one available. The most important thing for her was that we were all together and no one was left out.

Somehow, Twin Springs Resort came to the top of the list. A three-hour drive away, it was a good distance from the Twin Cities, not too far, not too near. It was outside the towns of Longville and Hackensack. I always remember where it was by thinking of the Billy Joel song, "Movin' Out," where he sings the line, "Who needs a house out in

Hackensack?" Of course, he was singing about New Jersey, but the catchy jingle made the cabin location easy to recall.

Twin Springs provided a fresh perspective on the whole cabin experience. Morningside had brought us together as a family for years, but we were all a little burned out on the place and looking for somewhere new. Despite having had a sneak-peek at the cabins on the resort website, we were still pleasantly surprised when we pulled into the driveway. The cabins were much more modern looking from the outside than what we were used to. Freshly painted with double-paned, tightly sealed windows, there was no sign of the neglect we'd seen creep in at Morningside during those later years. There were nine cabins total and our family rented several of them that first year in 1999.

* * *

One of the things I looked forward to at this resort was teaching my daughter Sarah how to fish. I'm told my father loved fishing and, naturally, my brothers and I all wanted to instill the love for the sport in our own kids. Prior to the trip, I'd purchased a Scooby-Doo pole for Sarah that would give her a taste of the fishing experience. She was not quite five years old, and I knew how kids her age had limited attention spans, so while I didn't hold much hope, I figured there was only one way to find out her level of interest.

At the same time, I wanted her to develop a healthy respect for the water. One of the rules we established early on for our kids was, if you were on the dock, you needed to wear a life jacket. This included while fishing. So, I buckled up her vest one sunny morning and out to the dock we went. Standing there dressed in shorts, a T-shirt, sunglasses, and an old baseball cap of mine, she was the dagger stuck firmly in my heart. She was innocence and cuteness defined.

The two of us tottered out to the end of the dock with my tackle box and a dozen worms I'd picked up in town on our way in from the cities. The dock stretched into the cerulean blue water of Pleasant Lake and had a couple of rental boats tied up to its supports. High, billowing clouds drifted lazily overhead providing momentary respites from the sun and heat of August.

I plucked a writhing worm from its nest of dirt and decay, broke off about an inch of it, and threaded it onto the small hook.

"Okay, sweetie, I'm going to cast it out for you," I said.

"No, Dad. I do it!" Ever since her days as a toddler, Sarah had an independent spirit, wanting to master everything on her own. I bucked this attempt knowing a flying hook was at stake, intent on teaching her the mechanics of a good cast

"No, no honey. I'll throw it out the first couple times, then you can try, okay?"

"Okay," she replied.

"Now watch how I do it. First you push this button here and hold it until you're ready to cast. Then when you throw it out there, you let go of the button, like this," I said, as I flung the line out into the lake.

I handed her the rod and continued, "Watch your bobber, now. When it goes under the water it means you have a fish, so reel in really fast."

Sarah stood there patiently and within ten seconds the bobber plunged under the water.

"You got one, honey. Reel it in!" I said.

She reeled furiously, the tiny rod bending at the weight of the fish. When she had it near the dock, she lifted the small Sunfish out of the water. Her face lit up like I'd never seen.

It was her first catch and, judging from her excitement, it was she, not the fish, who was ultimately hooked.

"Look sweetie, it's a Sunfish!" I said.

"Oooh, can I touch it, Dad?" she asked.

"Sure. Here, let me get the hook out first."

I wiggled the small hook out of the fish's lip and held it for her. She reached out and touched the scales on the bright yellow belly.

"It's slippery!" she said with a giggle.

"Yep. Okay, now you have to give it a kiss before I let it go," I teased, holding the fish near her face. She feigned a kiss, then I did the same and dropped it in the lake to fight another day.

"I want to catch another one, Dad."

"Yep, let me get you a new worm hon, and we'll try again."

I baited another worm onto her hook, cast her line out, and handed her the pole again. After ten seconds, her bobber started twitching and running laterally in the water. This time she didn't need my prompt, she started reeling frantically as the fish struggled on the other end. "I got another one, Dad," she said proudly.

"Yes, you do, Sarah. Great job!"

She lifted it from the water and into my direction. I unhooked it, made her do the fake kiss routine again and dropped the bluegill into the lake.

Over the course of the next hour and a half, this process continued until the community of fish got wise to it all and stopped biting. In that time, she'd caught more than thirty fish, none of them longer than four inches. She also managed to learn how to cast her line out, making my job easier. Sarah was a self-starter from birth, a highly-driven overachiever. Her trademark phrase was uttered numerous times that day on the dock.

"I do it!"

And to her credit, she had done it. She learned to cast, she learned patience, when to reel in, and several other subtle nuances behind the art of fishing. Over the course of the week, she spent hours crouched down at the end of the dock, Scooby-Doo pole in hand, pulling in bluegills as fast as I could take them off. As an avid fisherman myself, I couldn't be prouder of what was happening. Without trying very hard I was instilling the love of an outdoor sport in my daughter. Furthermore, I understood the excitement in her heart. I'd been there myself years before in Hibbing. Later the deal was sealed when my brother Tom gave me my first tackle box and took me fishing on Lake Phalen in the Twin Cities. I've been at the sport ever since.

For myself, perhaps the biggest thrill of the sport is the unknown. No one knows what lurks below the dock or the boat. No one knows how big the next fish you catch will be, or what species. Are they biting today, or not? All these intangibles add up to the eternal mystery that keeps fisherpersons coming back for more. It's a strange, inexplicable obsession or, I daresay, affliction, which stays with a person throughout their lifetime.

There was a big part of me that knew this week at Pleasant Lake, at our "house out in Hackensack," was where my daughter developed her love for the sport. She'd become one of the fishing brethren. It warmed my heart to think how proud my dad would be seeing her crouched on that dock for hours bringing them in. And I had no doubt, if he was still alive, he'd be out there with us cheering her on.

* * *

My brother Rob raised his girls with an equal love for the outdoors and for all things fishing. His eldest, Alison, to this day is happiest when she is outdoors with a fish on the line. This love for the sport most often, though not always, starts at a young age in people. I said earlier that what draws people in is the wonder of the unknown. Big fish? Small fish? Bluegill, or bass? It is for these same reasons one of my favorite games as a kid at carnivals or festivals was the fishpond. Just put your line over a curtain and when you feel a tug, lift it, and see what you got. It's a strange obsession, but there are a lot worse things kids could be passionate about.

Every summer, the town of Hackensack held a weekly fishing contest for kids on the municipal pier. When Rob and I heard of it, we thought it sounded like a great opportunity to engage our daughters, both under the age of five, in an activity they loved. Even better was the thought that we could do it in a friendly, competitive environment and maybe even win something.

On the morning of the contest, we loaded them into Rob's truck and headed into town. The girls were close in age, and this would be the first of many fishing outings they would embark on over the course of their lives growing up together. There was an excitement and buzz in the truck as we pulled up to the nearly full parking lot at the pier. Rob and I both looked at the crowd formed on the dock, then at one another, and raised our eyebrows grinning a grin that said, *oh my God, what have we done?*

"Little crowded," I said, sarcastically.

Rob pinched his index finger and thumb an inch apart and said, "Just a bit."

We both laughed. Young fatherhood had taught us that raising kids is no easy task under normal conditions. Throw a crowd, some rules, and a side of chaos at a parenting situation and it can be nothing short of exhausting. The stark difference between how we pictured the event and how it actually panned out became strikingly clear as Rob put the vehicle into park. We both smiled that knowing smile. We knew what we were about to undertake would create forever memories, but would likely involve three hours of baiting hooks, releasing fish, and trying to keep our daughters' attention focused. It was all good, especially given the knowledge we'd be able to laugh about the whole ordeal over a couple of beers at the cabin later that evening.

We piled out of the truck, unbuckled the girls from their car seats, grabbed our gear, and walked over to the registration table. The coordinator took the girls' names and ages and reminded us that life preservers were required for all kids. They also said the rules would be explained at the start of the event at 11:00 a.m. Rob and I nodded our acknowledgment and made our way out to the dock to stake our spot.

We found an opening midway down the dock and settled in. At eleven o'clock the main judge called for everyone's attention to go over the instructions.

"Okay, everyone, there are just a few rules to the contest. It will run until 12:30. All fish caught must be brought to the recording table so we can tally numbers and sizes. At the end of the contest, we will have prizes for the first fish caught, as well as the most, the largest, and even the smallest. There will be consolation prizes as well."

Because of Rob's hearing loss, I explained the rules to him after the judge finished. When I got to the part about bringing the fish to the judging table, he raised his eyebrows, much like I had done during the rule rundown. From a fish health perspective, it seemed like a sketchy procedure, to say nothing of the potential traffic issues on the dock. At the same time, I understood that to be fair, the only way to count and record the fish would be visual proof. *We'll see how this goes, I guess.*

As a safety precaution to the start, the judge reminded the crowd overhead casting was not allowed. The thought of thirty to forty hooks flying through the air at the same time was, frankly, horrifying, so thank goodness for small mercies. That would be nothing short of asking for an emergency room visit. It was clear that no overhead casting was the most important rule of all.

At eleven o'clock the official called out the start. Immediately every kid on the dock dropped their line into the water. After less than a minute, a kid down the dock hoisted the first fish of the day, eliminating that prize category almost before it started. Rob and I watched as our girls stood waiting for a fish to bite. With other kids to our immediate left and right, we had concerns about crossed lines. It was one thing to untangle your own kid's line, but no one is keen on the idea of having to untangle it from a neighboring participant.

Ten minutes later, Sarah's bobber went under.

"You got one, Sarah! Reel it in," I said.

Sarah cranked the Scooby reel and brought the bluegill out of the water.

"Yay, Sarah! Swing it over here so I can take it off."

I took the wriggling bluegill off the hook and made my way up the dock to the judging area. When I arrived, there was a person ahead of me getting their own fish recorded. I stood patiently, fish in hand, thinking to myself, *well, this is about as dumb as it gets.*

When my turn came, I stepped up to the table and said, "Sarah Landwehr, one fish."

"Okay, got her. Thank you," the judge said.

To their credit, they were quick about the recording process. I thanked the judge and turned away. At the first opportunity I dropped the fish back into the lake. I walked back to our spot to find Alison reeling in her first catch. Rob beamed with pride as he worked on getting the hook out. As he got it off the hook, I grinned at him and said, "The line starts right over there, bud," pointing to the judging table. It was by far the busiest place on the dock at the moment. Rob looked at me again with raised eyebrows and made his way toward the judging table.

He came back and said, "Well, this could be a long day."

I laughed and nodded my head.

As quickly as I could get Sarah's hook baited and, in the water, she had another one on.

"Got one, dad!"

She pulled it in and swung it toward me. It looked remarkably like the previous one, as well as the one Alison had just caught. "Hey, nice one, sweetie." I crouched down, unhooked it, and made my way up the dock to the judging area. Again, there was someone ahead of me in line. Again, I saw both the absurdity and necessity of the process. I registered it, set it free, and returned to our spot.

This controlled and measured insanity continued for the next hour and twenty minutes.

Catch, carry, record, release, repeat.

Forty-five minutes into it, Alison's interest began to wane, forcing Rob to tend her line while she watched. Five minutes later, Sarah followed suit and I was forced to tend hers. It seemed the kids contest had turned into an adult contest.

Rob and I were determined to finish out to see if one of the girls could win a prize. No one ever said fishermen aren't competitive.

The contest ended promptly at 12:30. Most of the kids on the dock had lost interest by then anyway, including a few who had left with their parents altogether. Rob and I decided to stick around for the awards ceremony to see what the winning numbers were, but also to see what the consolation prizes might be for the girls. The awards ceremony dragged on and on. There was the usual sponsor recognition and altogether too much pomp and circumstance. I half expected the Town board chairman of Hackensack to show up and say a few words.

So, we waited until the bitter end when the consolation prizes were announced. Our girls each won a coloring book and crayons. They were both well pleased with their prizes as Rob and I looked at each other with that sucker look again. We both should have known better and cut out when the girls initially lost interest. Live and learn.

Looking back though, this contest was a win in other ways for us. For starters, it gave our wives a much-deserved break from the rigors of motherhood. Add to that, the quality time with our daughters as well as some cousin time for both of them. And, finally, there was a shared experience for my brother and me. We were both new to this fatherhood thing and doing the best we could. It was our attempt to create idyllic memories for our kids, while exposing them both to a sporting pursuit we loved. So, at the end of the day, we were one daddy-date richer, and that to me was the real prize in this small-town contest. And I think my brother and our daughters would agree.

* * *

Nisswa was another town near Twin Springs Resort. Like many of the lake country towns in the area it catered largely to tourists during the summer season and featured plenty of gift shops selling vacation trinkets like can coolers reading, *what happens at the cabin, stays at the cabin.* These shared the shelves with T-shirts and hoodies bearing the town's name silkscreened on them. And of course, they all had lots of decorative boxes made of cedar, complete with the requisite majestic moose or black bear scene.

These shops are cookie-cutter and formulaic across the tourist industry. Part of the reason people go on vacation is to spend money they shouldn't on things they don't need. My mother and sister have a saying; on vacation, money isn't real, it's play money. At least their proclamation acknowledged the spending for what it was. Ultimately, there's nothing wrong with the practice, I guess. It gives people the opportunity to take a little piece of their vacation back home with them. Those sailboat kitchen magnets and pinecone duck centerpieces serve to take people back to that cute little store in the middle of nowhere. They are memory-evoking tokens of time and place that ultimately end up on the shelves of Goodwill in four years. This is only done to make room for new pine-scented candles, "Native American" moccasins made in Vietnam, or the much sought-after playful raccoon salt and pepper shakers.

Along with the souvenir haunts, these towns all seem to have their standard tourist-draw activities. Hackensack has the kids fishing contest. Other towns have things like Loon Days or Walleye Fest. These events come complete with parades, street dances and classic car shows. They've become traditions and have carved their niche in Americana. They come wrapped in small town schmaltz that tourists eat up and hold onto. Out-of-towners cling to the ideals these communities seem to have as part of their value system. City dwellers come looking for a place where the only siren they hear is the Friday, 9:30 a.m. tornado warning test. These towns provide the hope for that place, that lost innocence.

Our family heard about the Nisswa Turtle Race from the owner of Twin Springs. Mom and my sisters were always looking for a chance to check out the local shops anyway, so the opportunity to tie it in with an outing for the kids made it even more attractive. Nisswa was a forty-five minute drive from the resort, so having two reasons to go made the trip more justifiable.

We pulled into town just in time to pay and register for the race. The races are held every Wednesday afternoon and parking was at a premium because part of the main drag was blocked off for the turtle racecourse. Temps were in the low 80s, and the town was bustling for a hot Wednesday in August near the close of a long summer tourist season.

The race logistics involved renting a turtle for five dollars. The course itself was a series of concentric circles drawn on the pavement. The inner circle served as the starting area where the turtles would be set. At the signal, the turtles would be placed on the pavement and the screaming encouragement by the kids would begin. The first one to the edge of the outermost ring won the race. Second and third place finishers were also recognized, as was the official "slow turtle," the one who moved the least distance from the start.

We let Sarah pick out hers. It was then it occurred to me that setting these creatures on the hot blacktop might be a bit cruel. On a normal cool cloudy day, I wouldn't think anything of it, but the day was warm, and I suspect the pavement was ten degrees warmer. Once the thought came into my mind, I could not un-think it.

A crowd gathered outside the race circles. The officiant reminded the kids to cheer their turtle as they worked their way to the outer ring. At the signal, the reptiles were set down in the inner circle and the race began. Kids and parents alike started cheering, shouting, and clapping to get their contestant to do the one thing they are not known for: namely, moving fast. From a sporting perspective, it was one of the stranger spectacles I'd ever seen. One just doesn't see these kinds of things back in the cities.

A couple of the racing reptiles were nimble and fast, at least fast for turtles, anyway. My guess was this wasn't their first race and they just wanted it over with as quickly as possible. Either that, or they had hot feet and were trying to reach a cooler area. Meanwhile, my daughter's took a couple of steps and stopped. It seemed to have a case of stage fright. Despite all our cheering and encouragement, it just sat there deadlocked, staring at the screaming crowd. When it did move, its movements were slow and, well, turtle-like. As time ticked, a couple of the faster creatures were already near the outer ring and things did not look good for our home team.

After a few more seconds, one of them crossed the finish ring and the race was over. Sarah's reptile still sat there like a disinterested slug. It was never really in the race at all. In some respects, hers was true to its nature. Slow is as slow does. Sarah was a little disappointed until the race officiant found out who had the slowest and presented her with a button recognizing the slowest competitor. It was a consolation prize likely instituted to keep the dejected kids from feeling badly. Sarah seemed to take some solace in the booby-prize-in-disguise.

Whatever its intent, I was glad someone thought of it. We pinned the button to Sarah's lucky fishing hat. It only served to make our adorable little fisher-girl even more adorable. Though I'm sure the turtles would beg to differ, the whole event was an eclectic piece of good old-fashioned Americana. It was a nice distraction for the day and one of those bizarre things you stumble upon only when you're exploring those small towns while you're at the lake.

* * *

That same day, while we were in Nisswa, we did a little souvenir shopping. We took the kids into a gift shop and told them they could each get one souvenir. Sarah immediately gravitated to a small bag of polished agates. She knew right away that they were what she wanted, and they quickly became known as her "pretty rocks." The stones were her personal treasure and as we left the store, she clutched them tightly.

After our shopping, we returned to the cabin later that afternoon. The owner of the resort mentioned there was a nice sandy area for swimming located across the lake. He even offered to let us use the pontoon if we wanted to take a bunch of the kids. A little trip out on the lake sounded like a good idea, so I asked Rob if he wanted to take a boatload out for a swim. He agreed, so we rounded up a half-dozen kids and their lifejackets and piled aboard the big pontoon. My wife Donna also came along for the ride.

Rob took the captain's helm and fired up the engine. I patrolled the kids as their youthful energy built to a roil. In a normal housing environment, the thought of watching over six kids would be nothing short of intimidating. At the lake though, things were different. Everyone was more relaxed, including the kids. I knew we were creating memories while also giving them some quality cousin time. All of this and a couple of boat beers for the adults would make for a day where a good time would be had by all.

Rob steered the Romper Room barge out across the broad flat waters of Pleasant Lake. In many ways, this pontoon was a perfect boat for kids. It would never tip over in the event someone moved too quickly. Its floor was spacious without curves to negotiate like those of the more tippy variety. Perhaps most importantly though, the whole deck was fenced in. Unless you had an unruly kid, there was little danger of one falling overboard.

When we reached the sandbar, Rob slowed the boat and killed the engine. It was deep enough you could see the lake bottom out of the front, but not the back. The older kids wanted to be able to jump off the pontoon, so we anchored in about five feet of water. One by one, the bigger kids jumped in. Unlike the beach at the cabin, this sandbar offered the chance to swim without the threat of weeds nipping at your ankles. Weeds are always the creepy drawback of swimming in lakes.

Sarah chose to stay on the boat with Rob, Donna, Alison, and me. She loved being with her cousins but wasn't crazy about the water at this age. This was more a trip for the middle-school kids anyway. Since she'd become very attached to her bag of pretty rocks from our trip to town, she'd brought them aboard. She set them on the deck as she leaned on the rail talking to her cousins Stephanie and Nick as they swam in the lake. Rob, Donna, and I talked across the boat in the shade of the overhead canopy.

Rob stood up to get a beer out of the cooler and as he approached it, he accidently kicked Sarah's bag of rocks. They fell with a plunk into the water. When he realized what caused the splash he'd seen, he looked over at me and Donna with a look of dread.

"Uh oh, I just knocked your rocks in the water, Sarah."

"What? What happened?" Sarah asked.

"Were your rocks sitting right there?" Rob said, pointing.

"Yes. They fell in?" Tears began to well up in her eyes.

Oh no, this is not going to be pretty.

Sarah's affections as a child were always intense for things she treasured. She wasn't big on accumulating a lot of toys or possessions, but those few she had were sacred to her. What just transpired rocked her to her core, literally in this case.

"My pretty rocks!" she said, through a torrent of tears.

"Oh, Sarah, I am so sorry," Rob said.

She sobbed through her grief, muttering, "Muh, muh, pretty rocks."

Attempting to quell the developing flood, I called out to the kids in the water, "Hey, you guys, Sarah's rocks fell in the lake right around here. Could one of you dive down and see if you can find them on the bottom?

"I'll look for them, Sarah!" Stephanie volunteered.

She swam to where we were standing on the pontoon, then dove down. She was under the water for a few seconds and came up for air.

Gasping for breath, Stephanie said, "No luck. I'll keep trying though."

Stephanie loved her cousin and it troubled her to see her so upset. She dove again and came up empty handed. By the third dive, Sarah's grief had scaled back to sobs and sniffles, but the loss was still real.

I could see from his body language Rob felt awful. It was an honest mistake, and he certainly didn't want to be seen as the bad uncle. He tried to reason with her. "Sarah, I'll tell you what. We'll go into town and get you some new ones, okay? I'm so sorry I knocked them in."

"Okay. Thank you, Uncle Rob," she said with a sniffle.

It appeared we were all going to survive the pretty rocks incident after all.

Donna sat with Sarah and tried to comfort her. Meanwhile the kids in the water splashed and swam until the novelty of the sandbar had worn off. They all climbed back onto the pontoon deck and dried off with their towels. I pulled up the anchor and Rob started the motor for the ride back. The kids dug into the snacks and soda looking to replenish some of the calories they'd just burned frolicking in the water.

Lost rocks aside, the swimming trip had been a fun outing. I was proud of my niece for her efforts in the search for Sarah's treasure. It showed selflessness and compassion. More importantly, it was these cousin-to-cousin interactions that brought them closer together as extended family. Growing up, most of my own cousins lived an hour and a half away in St. Cloud, so I never really got to know them. These annual trips to the cabin were pivotal in the development and nurturing of family relationships that have only grown richer over the years. And for that, I am incredibly grateful.

* * *

Among the other diversions we'd heard about in the area near Twin Springs Resort was a petting zoo. Evidently there were deer and ponies at the zoo that were docile enough to approach and feed. As parents of young children, we thought it might provide a fun evening for the kids and their cousins. Sarah and Ben were five and two respectively, and their cousins, Alison and Hunter, were close behind in age. We consulted with the rest of the family and most agreed it would be a worthwhile side trip.

At the appointed hour, we loaded up our cars, vans, and pickups and caravanned to the petting zoo. As with most tourist attractions, I was skeptical of what the experience might be like. I'd been to enough places that only wanted to take my money as fast as I could get it out of my wallet, so I didn't hold much hope for a family park geared for kids.

When we arrived, we all regrouped at the entrance to the zoo. When you have more than a dozen people in your group, you instantly become a mob. Moving becomes more random and sheep-like. Some move slowly, others fast, and it seems there's always a few stragglers off in the clover somewhere. God forbid there is a restaurant meal involved. Those are nearly impossible to orchestrate without at least one emotional breakdown by either child, parent, or waitstaff.

At the entrance, we all paid for our various families and headed into the park. A walkway wound through much of the zoo, but most of the space was green. The terrain was undulating with several boulders jutting up from the ground giving some contour to the grassy landscape. There were about a dozen small deer and a handful of Shetland ponies milling about feeding on the grass or eating from the hands of some of the other guests. A couple of small play areas with swings and slides were set off to the side, providing an option to smaller, disinterested children. On the other side of a fenced perimeter was a mini golf course. Like many of the tourist attractions, this place aimed to please at every level, all in the name of profit.

It wasn't long into our arrival before the deer began to approach us looking for a handout. I bought a serving of corn from the gumball machine dispenser, then handed some of it to Sarah. She closed her fist tightly and then slowly approached one of the does.

"Hold your hand flat honey, so the deer can eat the corn, Sarah," I said, in an effort to keep her fingers to a complete set of five.

The deer approached slowly, with hesitancy. Sarah extended her hand and the small doe nibbled away at the corn. Sarah glanced up at us with a big smile. She loved animals and we knew she was in her element. Little Benjamin watched with curious amazement. At two years old, this was as close as he'd been to an animal of this size. He looked on, pointed at it, and said, "Deer, mom."

"Yep, Ben. Sarah's feeding it, isn't she?"

He laughed his little boy laugh as we handed Sarah the other half of the corn for the doe. When we were done, we moved on to explore more of the zoo's creatures. A couple deer lay in the grass chewing their cud while the rest milled about grazing or following other patrons around looking for a snack.

We came to a small Shetland pony. They were used to human exposure, so they didn't flinch as we approached. This pony was more interested in the grass it was eating than the gawking tourists, so barely gave Ben a second look as he squatted down and pointed at the grazing equestrian. It was a tender moment between a small boy and a beautiful, equally small horse.

The whole scene was a little bit like a dream. The large boulders projecting out of the green grass carpeting the area; the gentle animals in coexistence with their human caretakers; the fading summer twilight; and our family sharing time together. All of it just swept me away. I am a bit of an escapist anyway, prone to dreams of idyllic places of peace, harmony, and happiness. This setting was all of that.

"Isn't this place cool? It's like a fairytale. I want to live here," I said to Donna.

She laughed and nodded her agreement. She's not as much an escapist as I but could appreciate the beauty and serenity of the moment.

After another half hour of feeding and wandering, we gathered again as a family and walked toward the exit. My cynicism about venturing out from the cabin to go to a tourist trap like this was negated by what I'd just experienced. Yes, it was just a deer park, not unlike Fawn-Doe-Rosa, a place we'd visited when I was a boy. But, for me, it was a magical place, almost Garden-of-Eden-esque. A place where humans and nature got along peacefully together. It sounds strange, but the place gave me hope. An idealistic hope for my children, that they may grow up to be gentle and respectful of all animals and creatures. A little part of me thought if this place is anything like what heaven is like, well, that would be alright with me.

* * *

Life at the cabin for parents of young children was a game of give and take. The goal was rest and relaxation for both parents, but that required tag-teaming care of the kids. The "tag-you're-it" mentality ensured that your significant other had their time free from the responsibilities of sippy cups, dirty diapers, and all the attendant feeding and watering those kids required. It was a mix of sacrifice and duty in the name of happy spouse, happy house.

It became evident early on in my fatherhood experience that the days of extended fishing outings with my brothers at any cabin came with new parameters. Leaving a child or two in the care of your wife on short notice while you went out in a boat fishing and drinking beer was just something no sane man would attempt without express written consent. No. The obligations brought on by these little bodies required carefully scheduled escapes. The collaboration between brothers usually took place beforehand to get the date, time, and specifics of fishing departure solidified, all the while ensuring pre-trip brownie points were sufficiently tallied. Furthermore, this request for guy-time included a well-defined ETA and reciprocal provision for equal alone time for the spouse. It also required focused attention to the duties of fatherhood throughout the week. It was a gamble in hopes that when the fishing requests were made sufficient credits in selflessness were accumulated to justify time in a boat with a brother or two.

During the trip in 2000, Rob and I arranged to go out later in the week. We'd had an outing earlier in the trip and wanted to get one more serious fishing effort under our belts. As busy fathers working our way up the corporate ladders, these weeklong vacations were often our only chance all year to get out together. Neither of us owned a boat, so the rental that came with the cabin served as our means to catch the trophy we'd waited all year to catch.

After dinner that night, we met at the boat and loaded our gear. There were rods, tackle boxes, a small cooler with a couple beers, and a pack of cigars covertly hidden away. The stogies served to remind us why we didn't take up the habit full time. Dreadful things, really. I've always said they are the vice you enjoy one day and then taste for the next thirty-six hours. It is the bad habit that keeps on giving. Yet I still look at them as part of any good fishing trip. And if smoking three cigars a year is going to kill me, well, pass the lighter. At least I'll die having all the dizziness of a good tobacco buzz, and the memories that accompany fishing in a boat with my brothers.

I primed the engine, pulled the ripcord, and we set off. We motored along the western shore looking for a spot with some decent vegetation. Ten minutes into our ride, I killed the engine near some emergent lily pads. Rob dropped the anchor and we started casting our Rapala lures in hopes of catching something, anything.

As we fished, we talked about our lives. I was nearly four years into a new job at Waukesha County in Wisconsin, and Rob had a good position with the State of Minnesota. He worked for the gaming commission as an information technology administrator. Both jobs had their share of related stress, so chances to relax like we were this evening were a welcome relief from those responsibilities. I stoked up one of my Backwoods cigars and offered one to Rob. He took it, lit it, and puffed until the end was glowing amber.

At some point we started talking about the family, both the immediate and extended Landwehr clan. After a few recollections of various dysfunctions, addictions, and general familial fuckups, I said, "Yeah, our family has just a hint of hillbilly redneck in it doesn't it?"

Rob broke out laughing. He pinched his thumb and index finger a half-inch apart and said, "Just a little."

For some reason, his quick comeback brought me to uncontrollable laughter. The release was positively therapeutic, a letting go of the everyday stress of jobs, mortgages, and parenthood. It set the stage for even more humorous exchanges of stories between us about family and friends. This included people we loved who seemed stuck in bumbling cycles of bad choices and ill-informed decisions.

While we laughed and smoked and cast, it occurred to me we weren't laughing in mockery. Rather, our amusement was coming from a deep well of love for family. Rob always held family first, as did I. But it was this exact quality, this caring, empathy, and mutual respect that frustrated us. We genuinely cared about those drifting from the lanes of relative health, normalcy, and happiness through their bad choices and an apparent inability to correct their course. We loved them and wanted them to succeed. But we also knew we could not live their lives for them, nor intercede on their behalf. These friends and family would have to figure it out for themselves.

This is not to say Rob and I had it all figured out. We had our share of setbacks and bad decisions in life too. We also knew our suburban, picket-fence lives were not for everyone either. But we both knew the adversity our family, and specifically our mother, had gone through based on some poor life choices by our father and stepfather. We knew life required a series of ongoing checks and balances on behavior patterns and subsequently taking corrective actions, if needed. Life isn't rocket science, but it does require a little introspection and the occasional denial of self in the interest of others.

In a way, the boat we were sitting in was serving several functions as it rocked gently in the water. It was part psychiatrist's office as we took turns talking about our own childhoods and the role birth number took for each of us in our family of seven kids. It was part think-tank for strategizing how to solve our problems, or the problems of others, and laying out what needed to happen to fix them. The confines of the sixteen-foot boat were part health spa as we relaxed under the amber glow of an August sun and built up our immunities with a healthy dose of laughter. Laughter so convulsive, it almost hurt. And, finally, the boat was part mental ward, as Rob and I related we were both only one job loss from a vodka-bottle-under-the-bed condition not too far from those we joked about.

Our mutual love and concern for our extended family was played out that night as we shared our perspectives. We agreed that despite life's hardships, family should always be there to catch the fallen. The older we got as brothers, the more we came to understand what it meant to be there for one another. He and I had strikingly parallel lives at that moment and, if nothing else, it was nice to have a sibling there to cheer you on, to give advice if asked, and share a covert cigar under the guise of an evening of fishing.

There were no fish caught that night, and I guess that's okay. When it was all done, we fired up the motor and putted back to the lives we'd grown into, re-energized by the company of one another, and the time alone we'd had to work some of it out.

* * *

Toward the end of our week at Twin Springs, the adults decided they would take the pontoon out for a sunset booze cruise. It was to be an adults-only affair with the teenagers staying back and watching the younger kids. After five days of kids, swimming, and fishing, we all needed a bit of adult time. Time of relaxation, laughter and conversation. It was largely Mom's idea, as she hadn't been out on the water all week. It seemed to her like a good chance to see a little of the lake.

At the appointed time, Rob took the captain's chair. My mom climbed aboard as did my wife, sisters, and sisters in-law. Everyone took their seats around the perimeter of the pontoon deck. A cooler full of beverages was loaded, as were a few bags of snacks and the can of bug spray that seemed to travel everywhere during the week up north. In summers at the cabin, people practically carried mosquito repellent in holsters as defense against the bloodsucking pests.

Once everyone was situated, we powered out onto the open water. The lake was calm, flat, and glassy. The sun hung low and warm on the horizon. People sipped their wine and drinks as we motored along at a slow, mellow pace. Some yahoos liked to blast around the lake at top speed in their overpowered speedboats and jet skis, but not this family. Jet skis are among the most hated machines among the Landwehr brothers. They were for frat boys and up north hillbillies, the equivalent of an air horn at a symphony. All four of us hated them. We always favored small fishing vessels, or low-and-slow boats like the party barge we were aboard.

Eventually we slowed to a stop once we were across the lake. I thought it would be a good chance to get a couple of pictures. I climbed over the front railing of the pontoon to get a good shot of the folks in the back of the boat.

"Hey, be careful, Jim! Don't fall in," Mom said.

I laughed and flailed my arms like I was going to fall.

"Whoa, whoa!" I said in jest to see if I could give her a fright. "Ma, I'm fine. I'm a big boy."

Mom laughed and disregarded my smart-aleck comment. It seemed the old adage, once-a-mother, always-a-mother, carried through even when your kids were nearly forty years old.

I climbed back over the railing and Rob continued to cruise around the lake. The family all sat back, enjoying their beverages and the calming effect of the water. We all knew these outings with family should be cherished because none of us knew when it might happen again, or who might be absent for one reason or another. We were all deep into raising families of our own and that sometimes came at a price of taking separate vacations.

An hour and a half into our trip, Rob turned the vessel back toward the cabin. Everyone had enough sun and fun. It seemed Donna had more of the latter than the rest of us. Her speech was starting to slur a bit and it became apparent she'd had too much wine. As we pulled into the dock, she mentioned she needed to go to bed. It was only eight o'clock, but I couldn't help but agree it was her best course of action.

"Hon, you need to go to the cabin and go straight to bed. Do not talk to the kids if you can avoid it," I said.

I'd not seen my wife in this state very often and I was a little embarrassed for her being so tipsy in front of my family. I mean, we've all been there at some point, and it is never pretty. To be honest, given the stresses of young motherhood, combined with the added pressure of a week with the in-laws, I can't say an accidental over-imbibing wasn't warranted. I certainly couldn't fault her.

I kicked into caregiver mode to get her safely home and into bed. I followed her into the cabin, reminding her to keep the conversation to a minimum. To her credit, she followed the script tightly. I told her I'd take care of putting the kids to sleep as she tottered off to our bedroom. The booze cruise had certainly lived up to its name. It was clear that, during "mama's time" to have drinks on a boat with family, she had taken full advantage. Again, it happens to all of us. No harm, no foul.

* * *

Being at the cabin sometimes brings out the little kid in adults. I know it did for Tom and me one hot August day at Twin Springs. The two of us and our kids were all on the beach swimming and horsing around. We spotted a couple of floating beach toys tied up to the dock. They were called Water Bugs, and they were hollow yellow plastic platforms with a rope tied to the front. With a double hull, they were meant for standing and could be used by virtually anyone from ages 10 to 70. The Water Bugs were propelled by shifting your weight from foot to foot. As the rider rocked the platform, it gained speed. Not great speed, but speed. After seeing the nieces and nephews on them earlier, Tom and I were unable to resist.

We both waded over to the dock and picked out a bug. Boarding the vessel was not an elegant process. I flopped onto the deck and then wriggled up toward the middle until I could get on my hands and knees. From there I grabbed the rope and tried to stand. At this point, the rope was the only external source of balance on the highly unstable craft.

Once we were aboard and oriented, the competitive juices started flowing.

"How about a race around the buoy?" I asked.

"It's on!" Tom replied and took off rocking back and forth on the unwieldy floating craft.

I set off in chase, screaming, "No fair, you got a head start!"

Tom only laughed and continued his manic rocking to increase his lead. The family on shore shouted encouragement as we thrashed in the lake.

I don't remember who won the race that day, though it probably involved an illegal push or collision. I do remember the competitive spirit I felt challenging my older brother to a race in a sport not fit for an Olympic pool. Tom is as stoic and as serious as they come, a product of our German and Swedish heritage. So, to see him shedding a few inhibitions and having a little fun was uncharacteristic. It seems we both had become little kids again, burning off energy in the name of a few laughs. From an outsider's perspective, it was probably as hilarious as it felt from the deck of the watercraft. Two tall, balding adults goofing off like no one was looking. For all the fun I was having, I didn't much care. Being at the lake often serves as a portal back to our youth, and Tom and I had certainly stepped through to the other side.

Spider Lake

Like an old friend
the dock is there to lean on
shoulder to shoulder.

Our vacations at Twin Springs Resort only lasted a few years. Again, Mom had some issues with the owners and one of her sticking points was she wasn't crazy about the beach area. It was a steep climb to the waterfront and less than kid-friendly, to say nothing of seniors. When Mom gets fixated on a detail like that, well, it's probably time to start looking elsewhere.

At the time, Donna had a friend she used to work with at Independence First, an independent living agency in Milwaukee. Her friend, John, was head of the disabled sports program that focused on wheelchair and adaptive sports. John left Independence First to pursue his dream of owning a resort in northern Wisconsin. He was always an outdoor sports fanatic, and the thought of owning a place where one of the requirements involved taking people on kayak trips and nature hikes was reason enough to change careers. So, he bought Pine Forest Lodge near Mercer, Wisconsin and has been running it for over twenty years.

In 2003, Donna checked the place out online and talked to John a little about the prospect of the Landwehr family renting a few cabins. The resort was a five-hour drive from our home in Waukesha. It was almost the exact same distance and drive from St. Paul, where my extended family lived. The idea initially met with great resistance from Mom when we found out we couldn't get the number of cabins we wanted.

"If we can't all go, it is a deal-breaker. The cabin is all about family being together. The *whole* family," she said. It was clear in talking to her about it on the phone she wouldn't tolerate anything less than complete accommodations for everyone. Fortunately, by some miraculous turn of events, cabins began to free up, enabling each of the families to rent their own unit for the week. Mom continued to be skeptical, especially considering the resort was in Wisconsin, not Minnesota. The fact that the whole family would be together though, made the decision easier for her. The search in Minnesota for a place that could handle the size of our mob was failing to turn up decent alternatives. She and the rest of the family all signed up for cabins at Pine Forest with the understanding that if it didn't meet everyone's expectations, we would look for a different resort the following year.

* * *

Pine Forest Lodge has a total of eight cabins, and an expansive main lodge which doubles as a home for the owners, John and Sherri. The resident cabins lined a main drive and extended all the way down to the broad, sweeping beach area and boat launch. The dwellings varied in size from a one bedroom all the way up to a three bedroom that slept up to eight people. The units were each named after a species of tree, with names like Birch, Alder, and Hemlock.

The cabins were spaced out far enough to give privacy, but close enough to impart a sense of community about the camp. Woods are where some go to isolate, others to gather.

Each scenario serves a different need with the common denominators being relaxation and restoration.

The first year we went up, 2004, Mom brought a couple of dishes that became perennial favorites among the family. One was stringy beef sandwiches. She prepared the meat in a crockpot before the trip and started warming it up as soon as she arrived. Mom's cabin became the center of activity that first night, and her stringy beef was not to be missed. It was made with onions and spices that made it savory and delicious. Served on small Hawaiian bread buns, they were a sort of beef slider. It was a perfect start to the week, as most everyone was tired and hungry from the road and cooking seemed like a lot of work.

The other treat that was part of the first night frenzy at Mom's cabin were her chocolate-covered, peanut butter Rice Krispie bars. These were frozen solid before the trip, so by the time we got to them they were still cold and crunchy. The Landwehr family has a long history of sweet tooths, so these were popular, especially at the lake where dieting takes a vacation along with the person. Tom was always guilty of sneaking into these bars early and often. As I mentioned, the lake brought out the kid in all of us.

There were other foods that became part of the cabin tradition, some of them tied to specific families and some more universally shared among the camp. One of the meals my wife and kids favored were pudgy pies. These could be made either sweet or savory depending on whether you were cooking dinner or dessert. They required a set of pie irons that were circular disks at the end of a couple of long, metal handles. The hollowed disks closed on one another like clamshells and were held tight by a clasp.

The pies were made by starting with a slice of white bread in one of the irons. From there ingredients like pizza sauce, cheese, and pepperoni were added to form a pizza pie. Others preferred ham and cheese, or even peanut butter and jelly. If we were going the dessert route, some favorites were peanut butter and Nutella, or marshmallow, chocolate and graham crackers for a s'more pie.

Once all the ingredients were assembled, the irons were clamped closed and set into the coals to bake. This required careful attention and frequent turning so as to not burn the white bread crust. Occasional checks of the pies meant releasing the clamps and taking a quick peek. When they were done and cooled slightly, they were just a small slice of culinary heaven.

Along with food, everyone had their own favorite beverage up north. With our kids it was largely the top 1/3 of a can of soda or juice box. The remaining 2/3 usually ended up getting dumped down the sink or sitting on a picnic table serving as an attractant for wasps. This forgotten beverage phenomenon transcends all generations, as I clearly remember my mother complaining about it as much as I did with my own kids.

The adults had their own array of beverages and cocktails at the cabin. Early on, my personal favorite was a Minnesota beer called Pig's Eye pilsner. It was a cheap, rotgut lager, but at the time I was drinking it for reasons other than taste. First and foremost, because it was cheap. My tastes for cheap beer hearkened back to my stepfather who used to drink Hauenstein and Blatz, both of which were as cheap as beer came. The other reason I drank Pig's Eye was because it was a local brew that not only reminded me of my hometown, St. Paul, but also supported their local economy. Later, when I discovered they brewed an amber version, I was ecstatic, as ambers are my favorite style of beer. Pig's Eye was several notches down from being a good amber, but, as I said, it was inexpensive, and that counted for a lot.

Pine Forest Lodge has the exclusive claim as the birthplace of a Landwehr-branded cocktail that became the annual go-to drink for my mom and sisters. I'm unsure as to whether credit for the actual conception goes to my sister Pat or to Mom. I do know it was born during happy hour on the beach around five o'clock one evening. Pat mixed a shot and a half of vodka over ice and topped it off with cranberry juice. As she sipped it, Mom asked her what it was she was drinking.

"Here, take a sip," Pat said.

"Mmm, that's tasty! What's it called?"

"I dunno. 'Tasty' I guess," replied Pat, with a laugh.

Thus, the Tasty was born. And for the next ten years, rather than calling it a vodka and cranberry, the drinks were simply called Tasties. It became a code word for happy hour. "I think it's time for Tasties at the beach," one of them would announce. This was a signal to the others to pour one of their own and toddle down to the beach. The drink has yet to be patented or mass-marketed for the broader world, but it certainly has a supportive base up at the lake.

* * *

John and Sherri saw to it that one of Pine Forest Lodge's camp traditions was to host a potluck dinner every Monday evening. It was an attempt to try and get the cabin families to mingle a little at the front-end of the week. The premise was simple: each cabin family was invited to bring a prepared dish to the main lodge at the appointed time. The dishes were all set on the lodge's long bar and folks were allowed to help themselves and find a seat either indoors, or at one of the several tables out on the deck.

Because it was our one week together a year as a family, I always looked at this event with mixed feelings. I've never been a real socialite to begin with. Throw into the mix sitting down to a meal with relative strangers and I guess it all seemed more an obligation than opportunity. It is absolutely no fault of theirs for trying, however. *It's not you, it's me.*

Griping aside, me and my extended family always managed to make an appearance at the potluck. We brought hotdishes, salads, desserts and sides of every variety. The kids balked at eating anything they didn't recognize and picked away at those they did. John always used his trademark root beer float as a dessert incentive for those same kids, and the adults for that matter. He and Sherri were gracious hosts, welcoming each family as they came bearing their culinary contributions. Try as they might from year-to-year, most of the families tended to circle in their own private clusters. Our family was as guilty as the rest. Oh, sure, there was the usual small talk between people while standing in line, but, outside of that, families stuck together and gabbed away.

While these potlucks may not have had the fully desired effect John and Sherri hoped for, at a minimum they brought our entire family together for a meal every year, a feat that typically only happened at major holidays. The meals gave us all the chance to catch up with our siblings, nieces, nephews and cousins. It was an opportunity to talk at a slightly deeper level and get below the surface of our lives. If that dialog was the only thing to come out of these planned gatherings, well, I suppose they were worth every bite. Oh, and John's root beer floats made them pretty worthwhile too!

* * *

At over 360 acres, Spider Lake is sizable. Named for its eight bays representing the legs on a spider, it was always an extremely tough lake to fish. Lord knows there are enough seasoned fishermen and women in the Landwehr family that, if there are fish to be found in any lake, we usually sniffed them out. Spider Lake proved to be especially challenging, not just for us, but for other vacationers at the resort as well.

After a couple years of futility, my brother Paul decided to change his focus.

"These lakes up here are all pretty good muskie lakes," he said.

"Well, that might explain why there's nothing else in Spider, I guess," I said, not really joking. Muskie are the state fish in Wisconsin and are known for their aggressiveness and for being voracious feeders of smaller game fish. At the same time, they are incredibly difficult to catch and are known as the fish of 10,000 casts. Some fishermen expend considerable effort over a lifetime hoping to catch one, only to come up empty-handed.

Part of the appeal of fishing for muskies is knowing that if you hook into one, it may be the fish of a lifetime. The species can grow to over fifty inches in length. In fact, the world record came out of Hayward, Wisconsin, ninety miles southwest of Mercer. The beast measured sixty-three inches long and weighed sixty-nine pounds, eleven ounces. Northern Wisconsin is home to some of the best fall muskie fishing in the world, so there was no disputing Paul's argument that they were perhaps a better target than walleye on Spider Lake.

Paul went all-in on his newfound pursuit of the Esox masquinongy, the Latin term for muskellunge. He purchased an expensive rod and reel to be used exclusively for fishing muskies. His setup cost nearly $300.00, not including any lures, which typically start at $20.00 and go up from there. Being a skinflint, I scorned his seemingly frivolous outlay on such a single-purpose rod and reel. Just the phrase, "10,000 cast fish" dissuaded my interest in fishing for them. I was in the camp of my brother Tom who always claimed, "When I go fishing, I really like to catch something." It was hard logic to argue with.

Because the rest of us brothers were all a bit cynical of the pursuit, Paul went out alone one evening in hopes of justifying his new purchase. It was one of the few species of game fish in the upper Midwest none of us brothers had ever landed, in part due to a lack of trying.

Now, I'm not sure where I was at the time, but evidently Paul hooked into a nice thirty-six inch muskie in the first half hour of fishing Spider with his new rig. He was within shouting distance of shore, and managed to get Tom's attention. Tom quickly jumped into his boat and motored out. Fortunately, he brought a camera and was able to get a photo of Paul holding the fish.

When Paul got back to camp, he found Rob and I and filled us in on all the details: things like where he was, what lure he used, and how the fish fought. He mentioned that Tom had snapped a picture. Paul said he wished he was closer to home so he could get the film developed at one of those twenty-four hour processing places. It would help him validate his fish to us skeptics. As it turns out, I didn't actually see the picture until years later when he scanned it and made it digital. It was a beautiful fish and, from a family perspective, a historic catch as the first muskie caught by the four of us brothers.

* * *

Paul's catch that evening sparked a curiosity and competitiveness in us brothers, but each to a different level. Rob was hit hardest. Paul had sold Rob on the idea he needed a baitcasting reel and a heavy-duty rod with some backbone to it if he planned on throwing heavy cat-sized lures all day. So, the day after Paul's fish, the two of them went into Mercer in search for a muskie rod and reel for Rob. They came back an hour later, goods in hand and a couple hundred dollars lighter in the wallet.

For those who don't fish, the difference between a baitcast reel and a spinning reel is akin to driving a car with a manual transmission versus one with an automatic. It really is like re-learning how to cast. The most important thing to remember is to keep your thumb on the spool throughout the entire cast. Then, when the lure hits the water, you stop the spool from spinning altogether or it will continue to feed line and create a rat's nest. These nests will test your patience and dedication to the sport and, quite possibly, your will to live.

The problem was, Rob was an automatic guy trying to learn how to drive a stick. He'd used spinning equipment his whole life. But, like any accomplished fisherman, he walked into his first baitcasting experience with arrogance and assumption. How hard could it possibly be?

That afternoon, he went out with Paul just to try out the new rig. I watched from shore as he threw his first cast and proceeded to let out a long string of profanities stretching at least as far as his cast, maybe further. Paul couldn't help but let out a bit of a laugh. Anyone who has ever used a baitcaster knows the feeling of despair and rage at being on the receiving end of a good rat's nest. I certainly remember my first one. I think I spent the next hour untangling the mess and swearing I would never make the mistake again. I did, of course, and still do on occasion.

The discussion between Paul and Rob varied in volume and pitch over the course of the next ten minutes. Paul tried to be encouraging and give advice, but like many things between the youngest brothers, Rob never liked taking corrective advice from someone younger than him. So, the verbal volleying went on and on. Shortly after he got the rat's nest fixed, he created a new one which drew more seething and harsh language. It was trial by fire in a small boat for Rob as he struggled to master the art of baitcasting finesse.

He didn't catch a muskie that first year. His fish came the following during an evening outing with Paul. Again, I don't know where I was when they brought the fish to shore, but evidently Sherri even rang the camp bell to attract people to the beach to see it. I may have been putting kids to bed or something, I'm not sure. Much like Paul's fish, they managed to get a picture of it. It was a bit smaller at thirty-four inches.

My sister Jane was not one to miss out on an opportunity. While she was in Minocqua shopping the next day, she found a t-shirt that had a masked, caped fisherman on it. Emblazoned on the shirt in all capitals were the words, MUSKIE MAN. When she got back to the cabin, she surprised Rob with it. He laughed and said, "I love it! Thank you." He wore it with pride, as he should. Like Paul he had that first muskie to his credit. Much like his fish, Rob had been hooked.

* * *

The muskie fever incited by Paul and Rob eventually began to burn in the rest of the family. Jealous of their catches, a few years later I set out with my friend Steve to catch one of my own, and eventually did in 2009, although not on Spider Lake. I talk about this catch in the Birch Lake chapter later, so I will save the story for then. In any case, after seeing pictures of that fish, my daughter decided she wanted to catch a muskie of her own. I totally understood the longing, so I looked for a way to make it happen.

In 2013, our friends, Steve and Jill, decided to come up to Pine Forest Lodge. Steve said he was bringing his boat along, so we'd have a chance to try a different lake and get Sarah a fish. While it was true Spider Lake had produced for Paul and Rob, the rest of us all knew how hard it was to fish Spider. Steve and I agreed the odds were more in our favor to go to a nearby lake where Steve and I had experienced better luck in the recent past.

I'm sure Sarah would have preferred to sleep in that morning, but like a true angler, she knew the best time to fish was early. So, she was quick to rise and get dressed in hopes of catching the hardest fish there is to catch. She and I met Steve and got the boat ready to head out to the nearby lake where I'd caught mine. We drove to the landing on what started as a cool morning in August with the promise of a scorching afternoon ahead. After launching the boat, Steve motored out, then killed the engine. He got situated and started setting up the sucker baits for trolling out the back. Typically, we trolled two suckers (a live bait fish from seven to twelve inches long) out the back of the boat. Then, one of us would cast lures out the front in an attempt to increase our odds of hooking into a fish. We needed all the help we could get when trying for the fish of 10,000 casts.

It was our intent all along to let Sarah have the first fish that bit on one of the suckers. To keep things interesting though, I'd brought along a spinning rod to allow her to fish for bass while we trolled around the lake. Muskie fishing is full of long hours where nothing happens, so I hoped we could fill some of that time with a little bass action. I told Sarah I would let her fish from the deck up front with my spinning rod but wanted to check it out with a cast first. I threw the twisty-tail bass lure out and started my retrieval. Almost immediately, I got a strike, set the hook and handed the rod to her.

"Here, Sarah, why don't you bring in this fish?" I said. I'd caught enough bass in my life, so I thought I'd give her the thrill of bringing it in.

"Thanks, Dad!"

Sarah fought with the fish while Steve continued to set up the suckers. Bass are known for their immediate, aggressive strikes, so I was glad Sarah was having a little action with the smaller, more prevalent species.

The rod tip arced like a drawn bow at the weight and fight of the fish. Sarah reeled furiously, excited to have something on her line. As it neared the boat, I looked over the side to get a look. It is every angler's instinct to try and see the fish in case it should snap the line before it gets hauled into the boat. When I saw it, I could hardly believe my eyes.

"Holy crap, that's a muskie! Get the net, Steve!"

"Are you kidding me?" he asked in disbelief.

Grabbing the net, he peeked over the side and said, "Holy shit, it is a muskie! Work it over in this direction, Sarah!"

Sarah led the fish into the net as Steve dipped and scooped it in, safely capturing it. All Sarah could do was laugh in delight.

"I can't believe it. I just caught a muskie!"

"Yeah, on the first cast with a bass rod, at that," I added for emphasis.

"Right!"

Steve freed the small lure from the fish's mouth. When he lifted it, we discovered it was a tiger muskie, a slightly rarer breed. It measured thirty-four inches from lip to tail.

"Do you want your dad to hold it for a picture?" Steve asked.

"No, I can hold it, that's okay."

I thought this was a funny question. If there was one thing I was sure of, she would not be denied holding her own muskie for a picture. She'd been holding fish for pictures since she was five, so this opportunity would not go without visual proof.

Steve passed it to her while I readied my camera. I snapped a couple of shots of her holding it with pride and a big, happy smile. I don't know who was prouder at that moment, her or me. Sarah was the quintessential fisherperson, and this was her finest hour.

It was one of those postcard or scrapbook moments between a daughter, her father and a man she considered one of her uncles. On that cool August morning, we'd all just witnessed an almost impossible event. A first-cast muskie using the wrong equipment by a young woman who wanted nothing more than to catch one. It was a Hallmark moment the three of us will have as a memory forever. It was also the type of scenario that would continue to stir in us the longing to go "to the cabin" for years to come.

* * *

Sarah's muskie left Ben as the only one in our immediate family without one. It was never a formal competition mind you, but rather one of those pesky little things you want to cross off your list of lifetime achievements. Graduate high school, get that first job, and catch a muskie.

In an attempt to get Ben a fish we went out to the same lake the following morning. A mist rose from the water as the four of us piled into the boat. Sarah wanted to come along just to spectate in hopes Ben would catch his first. Unfortunately, as often happens with the finicky Esox, the lake produced nothing. Not even a false alarm. Ben's catch would have to wait for another time.

In 2017, Ben, his friend Van, and me went out fishing for an evening using one of Pine Forest's rental boats. These boats were small and utilitarian and, while okay for two people, three made for a bit of a crowd. We didn't have much choice, so we made it work. I took the captain's seat in the back with Van in the middle and Ben in the bow. We determined our best chances for any fish was all the way across the lake through a channel known as the narrows. We'd had some luck there in the past with a few small bass and figured it couldn't hurt to try again. Earlier in the day I'd purchased a couple of large northern minnows in Mercer figuring those would be our best bet for tagging into a rogue muskie.

When we were settled and anchored, I hooked the big minnow to my line and heaved it over the side, keeping track of it with a large red bobber. Meanwhile, Ben and Van cast their lines toward the lily pads afloat near the shoreline. Given the fishing history we'd experienced with Spider Lake, our expectations were low. We talked about the pending disappointment we suspected would come from our efforts. At best we were hoping for a couple of small bass or maybe even a northern. Worst case, the evening would be good for some laughs and conversation in a boat with my son and his friend. Not a bad fallback plan.

To our surprise, after an hour of false alarms and futility, Ben felt a strike on his bass spinner, and set the hook.

"Hey, I think I got one here,"

"What? Really?" I replied.

Sure enough, I looked at his rod, bent and twitching as he reeled it in. He pulled it near the boat, and it became apparent it was no bass.

"Looks like you got a northern," I said.

I netted the fish and he brought it into the boat. After a closer look we determined it was not a northern pike at all. The coloring and striping made it clear he'd caught a small muskie. It wasn't longer than twenty-five inches, but at this point in the week, it didn't matter much to any of us.

"That's a muskie you've got there, Ben," I said.

"Yeah, I was going to say it doesn't have the spotted pattern of a northern. I guess this means I finally got a muskie," he said with a laugh.

"Yep. You know, Ben, my friend John has a saying. "A muskie is a muskie. Doesn't matter how big," I said.

"I guess that's true."

So, the evening fishing turned out to be a positive outing after all. I probably made too much of a big deal out of it, but that stems from my love of the sport. My brothers Paul and Rob, and later, my friends Steve and John had introduced me to these mysterious fish that were so difficult to catch. From there, my love for fishing for them became a late-in-life obsession. To see my son catch one unassisted made me proud beyond words. To have been there for both of my kids' first muskies, knowing I'd instilled in them a love of fishing, well, that felt pretty good too.

* * *

Much of cabin life in our family is about slowing down and reading a good book. So often in the busyness of life back in the city, books get relegated to the "when I have time" corners of our lives. At the lake, especially when the weather is less than ideal, there is nothing but time for reading. This meant most everyone packed a good book to fill in the edges of our free time. My wife, kids and I are all avid readers who sometimes have multiple books in progress at once. Sarah prefers thick fantasy novels that create strange, magical worlds inhabited by witchy characters and creatures. Donna favors more traditional fiction, while Ben and I gravitate toward the dark humor of authors like Vonnegut, Bryson and Hunter S. Thompson. Donna in particular has been known to burn through three or four books in a week at the cabin. She is most happy on the couch or out on the dock with her nose in a book. Everyone knows and respects her whims. We fish, Donna reads.

Most evenings, we'd put the kids to bed after a day of running feral, and Donna and I would spend time in bed winding down with a book. One year, the mattress in our cabin was a bit too squishy for our liking, so Donna chose to take the couch and left me to the bed with the substandard mattress. We were both reading in our separate places having put the kids down forty-five minutes earlier. I thought they were fast asleep in their twin beds in the other room when I heard Sarah call out, "Mom?"

"What is it, Sarah? Go to sleep."

"There's something in my room."

"There's nothing in your room. Now, go to sleep," Donna replied. We were both brutally aware of these techniques used to prolong their stay-up time, and this seemed like another false alarm intended to do just that.

After another five minutes, Sarah called out again.

"Mom, there's something flying in my room."

"Sarah, it is probably just a bug or something, now go to sleep."

"It's not a bug," Sarah answered with a degree of certainty in her voice.

Donna called out to me asking if I could check on Sarah. We frequently tag-teamed our parenting duties and, evidently, it was my turn. I got up and walked into the kids' bedroom. I didn't see anything out of the ordinary, so reassured her it was nothing, and left.

"What was it?" Donna asked as I headed back to my room.

"I didn't see anything. It might have been a June bug or something. If it was there, it's gone now," I replied and went back to my bedroom.

Five minutes later, Donna called out.

"Jim? There's something behind the curtain out here."

My demeanor quickly shifted from annoyed to an unpleasant feeling of dread. What was everyone seeing that I was not?

I got up a second time and went out to play the role of the strong and fearless husband.

"What is going on?" I asked with a hint of exasperation.

"There's something moving and scratching behind this curtain here."

Unsure of what to expect, I went over to the curtain and gave it a little shake. It was enough to free a small bat from its grip and into a wildly random flight pattern so typical of these winged mammals. Of course, this flight pattern has also been known to intersect with tall, non-winged mammalian hominids.

"Ahhh! A bat!" I said, as I dropped to a low crouch. My fear of bats is real and ranks right up there with snakes and spiders. This fear usually brings out some less-than-brave instinctual responses. In my case it almost always involves ducking as a form of tall guy self-preservation.

These reactions are nothing to be proud of, but consistently come to the surface in moments of unexpected danger, like this ravenous bat in-flight.

Donna ducked and quickly moved closer to the cabin door. The bat circled the overhead light with occasional random wild variations in both height and lateral extent. Its ability to avoid hitting obstacles yet still sustain a pattern of erratic zigs, zags, dips and arcs was nothing short of impressive.

As it continued its laps around the overhead light, I scanned the room for a weapon of self-defense. Near the cabin door I spotted one of the kids' butterfly nets. They were used throughout the course of the week to catch frogs, minnows and even the occasional butterfly. I wasn't sure if they were strength tested for bats, but at the moment it seemed like my best defense.

Hunched like a bridge troll, I crept over and grabbed the net. From there I pondered my counterattack. Do I try to catch it on the fly, or wait until it lands? The former seemed like it had all sorts of potential for breaking windows, knocking over lamps and the like. Instead, I decided to wait for it to land. Even bats need a break occasionally.

In what seemed like ten minutes, but was more likely two, the bat finally landed on the same curtain it had come from. It was the perfect location for capture, actually. The curtain would provide a soft spot for the net and the percussion of it hitting the curtain might shake the bat free and into it. I walked to the kitchen and grabbed a Chinet paper plate to serve as a cap to the net. It is amazing the tools one resorts to in the midst of a little chaotic panic.

"You stay by the door and get ready to open it when I catch this guy, okay?"

"Yep, got it," she said. Bat hunting was a team sport.

Sarah had gone silent by now, apparently drifting off as soon as the "bug" was no longer in her room. It is tough to say how she would have reacted if she knew it was a bat flying around. She was a fearless kid though and had a love for most animals. She used to take particular delight in my feigned reluctance in going into the small mammal building at the Milwaukee County Zoo. The building housed an extensive bat display that gave me the willies. Sarah, on the other hand, was fascinated by them.

I moved stealthily over to the curtain where the bat was clinging. With a carefully measured motion I slammed the net over the bat, provoking it to take flight into the net. I slid the Chinet plate between the net and the curtain, trying to contain my girlish squeals at the thought of it somehow getting out and flying at my face, or something similarly unlikely.

"Open the door, hon. I got it!"

I hustled to the front door and threw the net and plate into the yard making sure it was positioned so the bat could fly free. We shut the door and breathed a sigh of relief.

"Well, that sucked," I said.

"Yeah. It must have come down the chimney or something," Donna said.

"You're probably right. Just to be sure, I'm going to check that flue." I checked it and made sure it was shut tight in case this was some sort of homing bat or something. I didn't know much about the species but wanted to take nothing for granted.

We mentioned the bat to John and Sherri the next day and they agreed it probably got in via the chimney. We emphasized it was not a big deal, but John gave the cabin a good exterior check-over anyway to make sure it was sealed up tight. We had a good laugh about the fact that we were in nature and when you are, these kinds of things happen on occasion. This is not to say we wanted it to happen again, and it didn't, but rather these intersections with various forms of wildlife were part of the whole cabin adventure.

* * *

I was never a strong swimmer as a kid. Always a little afraid of the water, I was more likely to be found messing around waist-deep in the lake while my siblings and stepsiblings swam out to the raft to horse around. I'd nearly drowned on the Saint Croix River as a teenager and swimming was a skill I'd never really developed until I was well into my thirties. It was then that my sister in-law Jill taught me the concept of the back float. She reminded me the body will float if you let it and don't fight it. All that is really required is to lay back and occasionally sweep your arms forward and kick your legs gently. She emphasized the most important points were to relax and not panic.

Over time, I became proficient at the technique and the cabin at Pine Forest allowed me the chance to perfect it. When I combined the stroke with a front crawl as a change of pace or when fatigued, I discovered a new appreciation for swimming.

I've said it before, but Tom is the real athlete in our family. While I preferred ball sports, Tom preferred long-distance events. He's competed in numerous 10ks, marathons and triathlons. While I claim to be in good shape, his physical fitness levels make mine pale in comparison.

He was also never much of a sitter. When he was on vacation at Pine Forest Lodge, he liked to be doing something. As part of his daily regimen, he took long swims that oftentimes took him out to the island about 200 yards from the beach of the resort. Of course, for Tom that stretch was just a warmup, but I always marveled at the feat of reaching the island without the aid of a boat or flotation device.

One year, I decided I wanted to try and swim to it just to see if I could. Donna was not crazy about the idea but said if Sarah trailed me on the stand-up paddle board, she would be okay with it. Sarah agreed and after significant back float and crawl effort, I managed to make it out and back without needing assistance. It was nice to have her accompany me as a precaution so I wouldn't fatigue and end up drowning on a family vacation. After that initial success, my trek out to the island became an annual tradition for me. It was a confidence builder and helped cure my aquaphobia.

My wife is actually the swimmer in the family. At the encouragement of her parents to participate in a sport, she joined the high school team, along with her siblings. Despite her love of the sport, she never much took to swimming in lakes. She said it has to do with not knowing what was below her, and not being able to touch bottom without risk of hitting weeds. Plus, she knew there were muskies in the lake. Big ones! She had heard enough stories of them occasionally attacking a foot dangling from a dock to keep her firmly planted in an Adirondack chair with a book while the rest of us swam.

As part of my annual tradition, I entered the water fearlessly for another trip out to the island in 2017 knowing my ungainly, thrashing style would be more frightening than attractive to any muskie in my path. I waded into the cool, iron-rich water up to the critical point we all know just beneath the waistline. Then, I dove in and swept with my arms. The cold water was a shock to my system and reminded me of what it is like to be fully alive.

Once I surfaced, I rolled over to my back and began my float. I always looked at these trips out to the island as a fantastic aerobic, low-impact workout. While I was never formally trained in freestyle swimming, I was always in decent shape, trim with a strong upper body. Once I'd learned the art of relaxing in the water instead of fighting against it, I began to appreciate how beneficial the sport could be.

As I paddled, kicked and breathed, I looked up at the glorious sun and relished in the ability to dismiss the worries of work for a week. For the short term, I was living the good life at my poor man's health spa. It was mind-clearing. Five minutes in, I began to fatigue so I rolled over to begin my crawl. As I swept my arms forward, I suddenly saw a water snake out of the corner of my eye. It was about five yards away and was serpentining from right to left in my field of view.

Now, I'll start by saying that muskies are not snakes. And while I had no fear of a muskie attack when I entered the water that day, no one ever said anything about snakes. Snakes of any species might be my biggest phobia, let alone those proficient at swimming. You can blame my fear on too many Tarzan movies as a kid, but the fear is real. Once, on a nature center tour for middle school, my daughter volunteered to hold a big Corn Snake when the guide asked if anyone wanted to handle it. It took everything in my big, brave self to just smile and watch, instead of running screaming into the street.

Needless to say, I immediately stopped my forward progress in the water and began paddling in full reverse. The snake continued on its way harmlessly as all sorts of bad scenarios ran through my mind.

Is that a water moccasin?
Or is it just a harmless land snake?
Can land snakes swim?
What if this thing latches on to my face and won't let go?

The more I thought about it, the more absurd and awful the possibilities became.

I wonder if they have water moccasin antidote at the hospital in Hurley?
Is there such a thing as water moccasin antidote?

As I watched the disinterested snake swim innocently past, I came back to rational thoughts. I knew the thing was probably more afraid of me than I was of it, and that gave me some peace. Eventually, when it was well into the distance, I continued on my way to the island. So much for the guy who claimed to be fearless of the mighty muskie.

This encounter reminded me that I was still a city boy. The resort owner, John, as an avid snorkeler, probably saw these sorts of things several times a year and likely didn't flinch. I also realized part of the reason we go up north is to see and experience things outside our comfort zone, which I most assuredly had just done. In the end, if I'd looked hard enough, I could probably say it was a spiritual moment between me and the serpent. For now, though, my story stands at disaster averted, and that's the one I'm sticking with.

* * *

Pine Forest Lodge had a much better swimming area than any other resorts we stayed at as a family. It was situated between two docks and was gently sloping with no drop-offs, which made it appealing for all ages. When they were young, our kids spent hours building sandcastles on the shore or floating around the shallows on one of the stand-up paddle boards.

As the kids grew, the beach became all about swimming for them and their cousins. It was the perfect activity to help them cool down in the middle of the day when temps were too hot to fish. A sizeable raft bobbed about twenty yards from shore, a favorite destination for kids wearing life jackets wrapped tightly around their chests. The assurance of buoyancy made even the water-shy kids brave enough for a trip to the raft.

The floating oasis served as home base for a game I made up one year while I was out horsing around with four or five of the kids. When we were all gathered on the raft, I announced, "Okay, we're going to play a game called raft trivia. I'll ask each of you a question, and if you can't answer it, you get thrown in the water."

Titters of excitement went through the group with a couple of brave souls raising their hands immediately looking to be the first to impress me, the professor of this floating college of knowledge. I picked Ben first and thought of a question. I grabbed him around the midsection and asked him an easy one.

"What is the name of the dog in the cartoon Scooby-Doo?"

"Ummm, Scooby-Doo!" Ben answered, smiling.

"Correct!" I said and released him.

The kids around me on the dock laughed at how easy this first question was. Of course, it was just a diversionary trick on my part to get buy-in from the others, thinking they could easily answer any questions I threw at them.

"Okay, who wants to go next?" I asked.

Arms shot upward all around me. I picked my nephew Hunter, a year older than Ben. I grabbed him under his arms and asked, "What is the capital of Wisconsin?"

"Uh, I don't know."

"Buzz! Incorrect! The capital is Madison. In you go!" I picked him up and heaved him into the water while he protested about the difficulty of the question. He landed with a splash in the lake and surfaced, still protesting.

"I want to go next, Uncle Jim," my niece Alison said.

"Okay, here we go. How many Teenage Mutant Ninja Turtles are there?"

"Umm, four!" she shouted.

"Correct! Now, a follow-up question because you're so smart. Who was the sixteenth president of the United States?"

"Oh, that's a hard one. Umm, Thomas Jefferson?" She answered.

"Buzz! Incorrect. It was Abraham Lincoln. In you go!" I said and heaved her into the water amidst her complaints about the difficulty of the question.

This went on for about fifteen minutes, with the questions ranging from simple for the small kids to more difficult for the bigger ones. It was clear they took delight in themselves when they answered correctly and even a bit when they got it wrong and ended up in the lake. On occasion, the kids started to give intentionally goofy answers to make their cousins laugh even if it was at the expense of them being thrown in.

"Who was the first president of the United States?"

"Umm, George Bush!"

"Buzz! Incorrect." Splash!

"How many legs on a spider?"

"Five."

"Five? Nothing in the world has five legs. In you go!"

After they'd all been thrown in a few times, they started to rebel against me, the corrupt game show host.

"You need to get thrown in, Uncle Jim," Hunter said, grabbing my arm and trying to rally some assistance from his cousins.

"Help me, you guys," he pleaded to the others.

They suddenly swarmed me and began pushing and pulling me to the edge of the raft. I feigned fighting them off knowing it was only fair I take a dive for being such a cruel host. After a short skirmish and a final push, I fell into the lake flailing and protesting like so many of them had. The kids cheered and postured about having vanquished the evil raft baron.

It is funny what kids remember because, for the next couple of years I was always asked if we were going to play the trivia game on the raft. In a small way it was satisfying knowing that, for at least one part of the week, I was the fun uncle. All of us uncles and aunts had our time and activities with the kids, from fishing, to playing Uno, to assembling a puzzle. It was a chance to be goofy or hang out with an adult other than your parents for a few days a year on vacation. Even if they were an evil raft baron.

* * *

Camp etiquette for the Landwehr family at Pine Forest Lodge featured an open-door policy with regards to both kids and adults. That was part of the beauty of the place. The resort served as a large family commune for seven days. The kids roamed freely from cabin to cabin looking for one another. This always included a slammed screen door and the pitter-patter of flip flops down the gravel drive. In other cases, if a family needed charcoal or batteries, or just someone to talk to, again, the doors were always open.

I'd have to say one of my favorite morning activities involved grabbing a travel mug of coffee and walking down to Aspen cabin where Mom and my sisters stayed. The unit had a screened-in porch and, without fail, I'd find Mom sitting out there with her coffee. Before she quit smoking, it was where she'd sit and smoke. When she gave up cigarettes for good, it meant coffee, reading, or just watching camp come to life one cabin at a time over the course of the morning.

Often, Donna came with me, and we'd sit and talk with Mom for an hour or so. We were the family that lived farthest from her and the rest of the Minnesota clan, so this hour was a chance to catch up on a year's worth of family events. It was never gossip. Mom never tolerated anything like that. Instead, it was things like how our jobs were going, how the kids were doing and what the schedule was for the day ahead. We talked about stories told around the campfire the night before, fishing adventures with the kids, or sometimes about books we were currently reading. It was conversation about everything and nothing. It felt good to be able to do it uninterrupted without the need to be somewhere else. We knew before long we'd all be back in the cities running errands, answering emails and chasing our busyness from task to task. It was refreshing to slow down and spend quality time chatting with a loved one.

As the morning wore on, Rob usually wandered down and joined us, or my sister Jane would wake up and come out and sit for a spell. These new faces brought stories and topics of their own and it didn't matter. All were welcome on Mom's screen porch, and if your travel mug ran dry, she always had a pot of Folgers in the coffee maker. It saved a trip back to the cabin and gave us more time to chat with those that mattered.

These spontaneous, winding conversations happened all the time at the lake. They started randomly, grew and then dispersed. Even better, you never knew who was going to enter the sphere of your cabin at any given time. These spaces were relatively open forums often held over coffee, soda or beer. The people in them served as sounding boards for our souls.

I remember one such gathering in 2017. Somehow it started with my friend Steve, Paul and I in Paul's screen porch. We were just talking and having a beer and before long, my son Ben and his friend Van joined us. It was talk mostly about fishing, sports and our jobs. As usual when it was just males, the conversation always had a rougher edge. Cursing was certainly unregulated, although with my nine-teen-year-old son there, it was kept slightly more in check.

Eventually, the conversation turned to the cabin accommodations.

"Yeah, the water in my cabin gets hot enough to boil a baby," Paul said.

The whole porch busted out laughing at his tragically sick, though accurate description. We'd all had the same experience in our cabin, so knew exactly what he was talking about. Paul's caustic analogy caused a fair amount of eyebrow raising because it was so irreverently funny. The comment fit Paul's sometimes shocking sense of humor to a tee. He often said what everyone else was thinking but were too reserved to say. He cracked us up.

Although it was said almost in passing, it became a run-ning joke around our cabin for the rest of the week, and for a few years to follow, for that matter. Part of what made this so funny to Ben and Van in particular, was because they had been fishing with Paul earlier in the week. They came back to our cabin saying his running monologue in the boat was hilarious. In some respects, he was the crazy uncle in the family, though I mean that in the nicest way. Paul mixes a quick wit with the hard edge of his punk rock past to form a blend of humor that is shockingly hilarious.

To this day, whenever someone in our immediate family says "baby water" we all know exactly what they are referring to, and where it originated. Because we all know its source was loveable, albeit sometimes crass Uncle Paul, it always makes us laugh a little. It has now become an inside joke in the family, and it all happened because of that spontaneous gathering in a screen porch at Maple cabin.

* * *

Our weeks at Pine Forest were sometimes a little long for those in the family that weren't into fishing and boating. To shake things up, we sometimes went golfing. My sister Pat's husband, Kevin, and Jane's boyfriend, Todd, both loved the sport, so there were a couple years where Rob and I packed our clubs for a round of golf in the middle of the week.

Rob and I were much less accomplished golfers than Kevin or Todd, both adept players. The two of us were more like once-a-year hacks. Personally, I always considered the game a rich man's sport, and I was far from that. Like any sport it is a game that takes devotion and tons of practice to get good at it. I had neither the money nor the desire to pursue it beyond what it was for me, namely an expensive, highly frustrating sport. Only playing it once a year provided me with the perfect excuse for those drives I sent deep into the woods and water. In fact, I love the analogy that a good way to screw up a nice walk is to add a golf game to it.

Our outings on the links up north were casual affairs. We always rented carts and brought a small cooler with beers in it to keep our interest up. It may have been a breach of some course rules, but if there's one thing nice about golfing up in those parts, it's that most rules are taken as general guidelines or recommendations. Bad drive? Take another. Missed that putt? No one was looking, take another shot. The only real up north golf rules were, keep your smuggled beers low and dispose of your empties properly.

There were a couple of different courses we played. One of them was Eagle Bluff in Hurley, about a half-hour ride to the north. It is a gorgeous eighteen-hole course, in as much as a mowed carpet of non-native Kentucky bluegrass in the middle of pristine wilderness can be. We only played it once. When I got home from the cabin later that week, I realized my pitching wedge was missing from my bag. It turns out I'd left it on the edge of one of the greens at Eagle Bluff. When I called and asked about it, they were kind enough to mail it back to me. It served to remind me this was not how the pros did it.

The fonder memories come from playing a much smaller course in Mercer, Tahoe Lynx. This name reminds me of the naming convention used for most subdivisions back in the city. My boss once said subdivisions were named for the native species they endangered or eradicated. True to this model, in the few times I've golfed at Tahoe Lynx I've never seen a lynx while in the area.

Much of the appeal of the course was its affordability and the fact that during the week it was fairly easy to get a tee time because it was so remote. Like most courses, the Lynx was challenging in its own way. Rob and I tended to play from the fringe of one rough to the fringe of another using the fairway only as a guide on how to get there. The Lynx had its share of woods and wetlands to play around to make it even more challenging. The thing about golfing with someone who plays as infrequently as you do is that you can laugh at each other's shots without hurting any feelings. And, trust me, there was plenty to laugh about.

One year, about halfway through our round, I realized I'd left my pitching wedge at the edge of the prior green.

"Hey, Rob, I forgot my wedge back at the last hole," I said.

"What? Really? Geez, Jim. Can't you keep track of your clubs?

Recalling my track record the year before at Eagle Bluff, he certainly had a point.

Rob turned the cart around and started back toward the previous green. As we neared it, the two of us scanned the grass for any sign of my club. A split-second after we ran it over, I said, "Wait, there it is!"

Rob was hard of hearing, so turned to me and said, "What?" just after the back wheels had passed over the club.

"You just ran over my wedge," I replied, laughing.

Rob hit the brakes. "Sorry, bro," he said, then joined me in my laughter. One thing was sure, between my absent-minded loss of clubs and his sketchy driving skills, we would not be invited to the Tahoe Lynx Invitational anytime soon.

I picked up my club which, thankfully, was none the worse for wear. Knowing the caliber of my game, a little tweak in my pitching wedge would probably only serve to improve things anyway.

We finished the round over the next hour or so. This included one hole which required shooting over a wide wetland. Rob and I each lost a couple of golf balls to it, sparking uncontrolled fits of laughter between us. That hole and this course were unkind reminders of why, if given the choice, Rob and I would both take fishing over golf, any day. The game is as frustrating as any sport I've ever played. If there was one thing for sure, it was not going to affect my week of vacation at the lake, and I think I can say the same held true for Rob. It was, however, the perfect excuse to have a few laughs, share a few covert beers and scream around in a golf cart. Not a bad way to kill a morning.

* * *

I think it's hard to say anyone loved the whole cabin experience more than my brother Rob. He always revered family get-togethers, and like the rest of the brothers, was happiest outdoors, camping, hiking or fishing. Those weeks in August at Pine Forest Lodge brought those things together, leaving Rob squarely in his element.

In June of 2010, Rob was experiencing back pain. After a trip to the doctor, he was sent to the Mayo Clinic for an assessment. Doctors found a large tumor on his spine and said surgery would be necessary as soon as possible. Later that month in a series of long, grueling surgeries, they removed the tumor and performed reconstructive surgery on his spine using titanium rods, screws and a mesh cage. He seemed to be on a path to recovery when the cancer returned six months later in December. The oncologist reported the cancer had spread to his lungs and he was diagnosed as terminal with months to live. The reality of his illness and subsequent decline was incredibly difficult for me, my wife and kids and the entire extended family. Often, during my daily walk to work, I teared up and was overcome with grief from the weight of it all. After a courageous eight months battling the illness, he passed away on August 30th, 2011, at the young age of forty-seven.

Perhaps the biggest take-away from the whole devastating process was how it brought the rest of the family together. Through texts, emails, phone calls and visits, we pulled close and, in outward ways I'd never experienced before, expressed our love for Rob and for one another. It was eye-opening what a tragedy of this proportion could do to a group of stoic German Swedes.

Rob died on the Tuesday before Labor Day weekend. Donna, our kids, and our friends Steve and Jill were slated to go up to Pine Forest Lodge for the weekend. We were apprehensive about going considering the sad news but thought it might help to get out of town and process it all. The day after Rob passed away, I got a call from Mom asking if it would be okay if the rest of the family came up to the lodge too. She thought it would be appropriate to gather us all in a place that was special to him, to express our grief and celebrate his life. It turns out she'd checked with John and Sherri, the owners, and they not only told her the big Ironwood cabin was available, but they would offer it to the family for free. They did the same thing with a second cabin for Rob's wife, Jane, and her daughters. That is just the kind of people John and Sherri are. Their generosity during this time of great sadness was astounding.

We all met that weekend, just like we had years before. It had been four years since the whole family had been up together. Pine Forest had become almost too routine. Tom, Rob and I all had young kids and had decided to use our vacation time to visit different states together, wanting to expose our kids to other parts of the country. Given Rob's unexpected illness and passing, I am so grateful we made the break from the cabin for those years and traveled the country. It made the return to this familiar place even sweeter, despite the sorrow that brought us there.

In many respects, the weekend was a bit of a blur for me. I think when you are in the thick fog of sorrow, details tend to fade due to the pangs of sadness that file them down and take away their sharpness and clarity. However, there were some moments I will never forget.

One was when our friend Steve expressed his condolences to Mom, only to have her return them. Steve had lost his brother to pancreatic cancer the previous December when we were in the throes of grieving Rob's diagnosis. Mom had remembered that, even in the midst of her own sorrow. Later that night in the cabin, Steve made a point of mentioning how much it meant to him not only that she remembered but deflected her own grief by reaching out to comfort him. This is how support systems are supposed to work.

Another memory was when I was sitting on the deck having drinks with my family one evening. During our conversation, I mentioned I was thinking of getting a tattoo of a muskie as a tribute to Rob. I also mentioned I probably would never be able to work up the nerve to carry it out.

"Why not, Jim? What's holding you back?" Tom asked.

"I dunno. Maybe I will," I replied.

"Just do it, Jimbo. As Rob is testament, life is short. Why live with any regrets?"

I was surprised to see Tom so animated about the issue. It was obvious the brevity of life was on everyone's mind, and Tom was no exception. It just seemed out of character for him, in a good way. Needless to say, due to his encouragement, I did get that tattoo the following April and I haven't regretted it for one minute.

All weekend long, I never acknowledged the fragility of my emotional state until I broke into tears in the arms of my sister Jane while the kids played board games in the other room. I'd reached the pinnacle of my sadness and sorrow that weekend and being around family brought it all to the surface. For some reason, it felt different and more healing at that moment to shed those tears with my sister than it had even with my wife during the months before his death. And believe me, Donna and I shared a lot of tears together. Both women were instrumental in helping me work through my pain.

Then there was muskie fishing after dark one night with Steve, something we'd never done before. On two different occasions we almost lost a rod over the side of the boat. Both of us laughed about it being Rob's spirit in the boat playing tricks on us, something I still cannot entirely dismiss.

And, finally, I remember talking to Paul and my sister in-law Jane, Rob's wife, in our cabin on Sunday. Paul was dressed in a Minnesota Vikings jersey because it was game day. We talked about our weekend, muskie fishing and some old memories. It was one of those impromptu cabin gatherings I loved so much. Shortly into it though, Jane left. We assumed she had something to do. Only later did I learn she'd left because seeing Paul in a Vikings jersey reminded her of Rob who had a similar one. Seeing him made her feel like she was going to lose control of her emotions in front of us. It seemed everyone had their moment of crippling grief that weekend.

Other than these things though, the get-together was shrouded in memories and mourning. Nevertheless, Pine Forest Lodge was *exactly* where we all needed to be. We had all made a conscious effort to come together and remember not only Rob, but also what we still had as a family. We'd lost our sister at the age of five, then our father a few years later, and now our brother. But there were still six of us, including Mom, and we needed to lean into how fortunate we were to still have that. As strange as it is to say, this resort was a sacred place for our family and made for the perfect setting for reuniting and remembering.

*   *   *

One of the unique qualities of Pine Forest Lodge is its wheelchair-accessible cabins. Because of John's spinal cord injury, as well as his early career work at Independence First, he wanted to make his resort a little different than the average. After he bought the property, he set to work adding ramps, widening doorways and changing door handles, among other retrofits. His philosophy was disabilities should not get in the way of an up north cabin experience. He blocked out a week every year specifically devoted to hosting a group of vacationers with disabilities. His focus was primarily spinal cord injuries for wheelchair-bound vacationers, but ultimately, John didn't discriminate. All were welcome at his resort.

Through the course of that week, he took extra effort to ensure *everyone* had access to the kayaks, sailboat, and pontoon. This meant a fair amount of able-bodied assistance for helping load and unload people into the various watercraft. From the pictures I've seen, it looks like a week of selflessness and sacrifice by John and others to ensure a good experience for those who might otherwise not get the chance.

Able-bodied or not, John loved being on the water with people. Always up for an adventure, he was gracious about taking any of us out for day-long kayak trips. He had a few routes mapped out, each with their own degree of difficulty. Most involved cruising a river or stream system connected between a couple lakes.

In 2018 he invited our family on a kayak trip along with half a dozen other boats. Ben, Van and I were up for it, so John added our numbers to the total count. He then requested our help in loading all the boats into the bed of a big old pickup truck he used for just such occasions. Another couple cars tagged along with their own kayaks tied on top.

We followed the caravan through the twisty two-lane highways of northern Wisconsin. Stands of Aspen, Tamarack and Jack Pine whizzed by out the window as we worked our way toward our day-trip adventure. After a twenty-minute ride we pulled over near a bridge that marked our launch point. We helped unload the boats and John laid out the plan of attack, giving us all a general idea of what we'd be encountering.

"Okay everyone, we're going to start out on this stream that empties into a lake. From there it empties back into a river that will take us to our landing point. Let's stay together as a group, as much as possible," John said.

Ben and I paired up in one of the two-person kayaks while Van opted for a single. We pushed out into the stream and quickly came upon our first obstacle. Before us loomed a large concrete culvert that, judging from the size of the opening, would require us to lay back in our seats to avoid scraping our heads.

"Well, this looks interesting, Dad," Ben said with trepidation.

"Indeed, it does," I replied.

As we entered the culvert, it was positively crawling with spider webs. It was a scene right out of an Indiana Jones movie. I've never been fond of spiders, but I soon found out they didn't terrify me nearly as much as they do my son.

"Oooh, Dad, look at them all! I'm in hell here!" he said with a sort of maniacal fear in his voice.

I tend to see the humor in most things, so couldn't help but laugh at his proclamations of our situational doom. As much as he was a full-grown adult, he was still my little boy. The same one who was going to run away at age four because of something we denied him. He got as far as the garage before running back in the house.

"What's the matter, Ben? I thought you were running away?" Donna asked.

"There's a bee out there."

And that was the end of the vagabond life on the road for our four-year-old.

As we pushed further into the culvert, Ben continued to point out the big webs and spiders. It was his way of working through his arachnophobic freak-out. I have to admit the whole scenario made me a little uncomfortable too. Like Ben, my concern was for the ones that might accidentally drop into our boat. We'd both seen enough bad spider bite pictures on the internet to know we were tempting some sort of funhouse fate in this den of eight-legged man killers. We paddled toward daylight and emerged, frantically checking ourselves for unwanted hitchhikers.

"Well, that was fairly traumatic," I said.

"Yeah, it was! The stuff of my nightmares," Ben replied.

Van had paddled the gauntlet behind us and laughed at our remarks as he made his way alongside us after his exit. We pushed ahead to keep the way clear for those coming up behind us. There was a small current in our favor, but nothing significant. It made for easy progress and plenty of time to take in the scenic beauty. A half hour later, the stream widened out to a broader body of water. It was a welcome change from the relative confines of the stream. It's hard to have a bad day on vacation in a kayak, and at this point I was feeling pretty good.

After a few more minutes, we came to a significant narrowing of the stream. It seemed to almost disappear into a field of reeds.

"Wow, the water is really down. This was all a lot wider open a few weeks ago," John said.

"Where does this go?" I asked.

"It connects to a lake, eventually," John answered.

He was the tour guide, so we had to take his word for it, despite what looked like an impossible passage.

Following those in front of us, we pushed into the reeds. The water was only a couple of feet deep in places and the vegetation was as thick as I had ever paddled in. Our paddles were continually obstructed by the lily pads and prevented any kind of consistent rhythm. Reeds scraped along the sides of the kayak reminding us this was their habitat, not ours. They slowed down our snail-like progress. Eventually, we wandered too far out of the main channel and came to a complete stop. We were mired in the mud and reeds.

"Dad, we're bottomed out here," Ben said.

"Yeah, I think we went down a blind alley. Let's try backing up and going more to our right. I hear voices coming from that direction," I said, pointing off into the unknown. We started paddling in reverse until we managed to free ourselves into slightly deeper water. Van and all the others had dropped out of sight behind the tall reeds.

"Van, where you at?" Ben shouted.

"I'm over here. I think you're still ahead of me," he called out from our right side.

While I wasn't scared, the inability to see or track the rest of the group was a little disconcerting, even for me, a seasoned paddler. We were in our own little private Amazon adventure and, while part of me was digging it, another part was hoping to get free of the "Wooly Swamp" that Charlie Daniels sang about so long ago.

When we were back in the main channel, we slogged our paddles through the lily pads occasionally lifting our blades only to find them covered in mud. To add to the fun, some of the reeds had spiders of their own. Not life-threatening, but yet another variable we needed to keep in mind on our quest to reach open water.

"Well, this is sort of a fresh hell, isn't it?" Ben said.

"Yep, sure is," I added.

After ten more minutes of hard paddling and navigational guesswork, we emerged from the reeds into the outlet to the lake.

"We made it!" I said.

"Well, that was fun. Or, not," Van added as he pulled up next to us.

We laughed at his assessment and paddled happily unburdened into the big lake. It felt good to move unfettered in a straight line as we once again progressed in relative synchronicity. If there is one thing I love about kayaking it is the sense of control and efficiency. Despite a punishing north wind, we followed John and the rest and managed to make it across the lake back into the river system.

After a short paddle down the river, we saw the other boats in our party begin to pull over to the shore at the bridge. The approach to the bridge was stacked with signs warning of the dangers that lay ahead. I don't recall the exact message, but they were explicit. *Dam ahead. Dangerous! Do not pass this point!*

"This must be where we pull out," I said.

"Yep, looks like it. I'm ready," Ben added.

The current in this section of the river was markedly stronger than we'd paddled in all day, and we were beginning to feel it.

"Hard right, Ben."

"Yep."

As we neared the bridge, our tail end started to drift and get caught in the current. I back-paddled attempting to prevent further drift. Despite my efforts, we started slipping past the exit point of the river and were now at the shore, but underneath the bridge. I heard the rush of water in front of us which signified a drop from the top of the dam to the new water level below it. None of us knew the height of the drop, nor wanted to find out the hard way. The sound heightened my concern as we fought for position against the current. Van, who was behind us, suddenly bumped into our boat making a dicey situation even dicier.

"Sorry, guys," he apologized.

"No problem, but we need to back up without getting caught in the current and going over the dam. Van, if you can back-paddle slowly and get out from underneath this bridge, we'll try and do the same. Keep your back end tight to the shore, though," I said.

"Yep," he replied confidently.

Much of what drove the fear welling up in me was the unknown of what lay ahead. All I could see was the river, but I knew the sound of rushing water brought bad things with it. I'd never been over a dam, and it certainly wasn't on my bucket list.

Ben and I worked in tandem to ease the kayak backward a yard at a time. A few near-misses later, we were at a point where Ben could get out and pull us safely to shore. As he did, my racing heart was a reminder we'd dodged a bullet.

Thanks in part to the strength and teamwork of the three of us, we'd managed to avoid a disaster.

"Well, that was sorta close, eh?" I said.

"I guess, man!" Ben said.

Van laughed and nodded. Tired from our long day's paddle, we hauled our boats up the steep bank and waited for our party to come back with John's pickup so we could load them in. During our wait, we went across the highway to see what the dam looked like from atop the bridge. We were surprised to see it was less daunting than it sounded from inside our kayaks. The vertical drop was no more than five feet or so, and while I am grateful we didn't end up traversing it, it certainly wouldn't have been fatal. Embarrassing? Yes. Fatal, probably not.

After a fifteen-minute wait, the truck and its crew showed up and we loaded all the boats into the bed.

"You guys feel like stopping for a beer?" John asked.

"That actually sounds really good!" I answered.

"There's a cool little bar near here and the guy lets us use his launch all the time. I like to give him the business. That way, our arrangement is mutually beneficial."

We rode back to our cars parked at the starting point. From there we caravanned to the bar. Like most bartenders up north, the guy was happy to see a crowd knowing he'd sell some beer and make some tips. Our party took turns ordering and we all found spots to sit at the bar or around tables. We sat and talked about our adventure, and as with most, they got a little richer with each telling. We'd had a good day on the water and now it was our chance to relive it and relax.

While it is easy to discount this trip as just another kayak ride, I think it falls as part of a larger work called a full life.

I love my kids more than anything, so shared experiences like this mean everything to me. We've always been a family that loves the outdoors, and it seems to have become part of our fabric. As we encounter the multitude of adventures in wide-open spaces, all it takes to remember them are things like a culvert full of spiders, or a close encounter with a small dam.

* * *

Our vacations at Pine Forest Lodge were, without question, the most treasured and memorable for me and my extended family. While many of us have traveled far and wide all over the country, these days spent with family among the trees and lakes of northern Wisconsin rest deep within the soft, tender part of our hearts. It is where our kids grewup and developed a love for family, the great outdoors and adventure. The years spent there have created storehouses of memories from which to draw upon as we all move through the busyness of the rest of our lives. It is also a place we can all someday return to with the knowing that we are always welcome. Pine Forest defines the best of everything that life can be up at the lake.

Uchi Lake

Last cast before dark
one last cast for a walleye
stalking the reef.

As a graduation gift to my friend Steve for completing his master's degree, his wife Jill gave him a fly-in fishing trip to Canada in 2006. Because he and I were friends, Donna had collaborated with Jill in advance for me to accompany him. When she brought it up to me, I was both ecstatic and, admittedly, a little apprehensive. The thought of a fly-in trip to Canada thrilled me. At the same time, while we were friends, he and I never traveled together before, let alone just the two of us for four days. Being an introvert, there were parts of me that panicked at the thought of having no third person to fill the silence when the two of us ran out of things to talk about. I realize these are weird and unnecessary fears, but I also cannot help where my brain takes me sometimes.

When Steve asked about where to go, I mentioned I'd heard from my brother Rob about a fly-in resort on Uchi Lake, in Ontario. He'd gone a couple of years prior and said he'd had a great time. Not knowing any better options, Steve and I booked a weekend near the end of June in 2006. With the date set, all that was left was the wait.

Steve and I drove twelve hours from southeast Wisconsin and stayed overnight in the town of Sioux Lookout, Ontario. It was the location of our water port from where our float plane was to depart. The following morning, we drove to the water port headquarters an hour before our flight was supposed to take off. We checked in, were shown where the plane was and told where to put our gear on the dock. The plane was a beautiful single-engine Otter painted in orange with yellow detailing. Seeing it made the long-awaited idea of our forthcoming adventure suddenly very real.

Another couple of guests stood on the dock with Steve and I as takeoff time approached. All of our gear was weighed to ensure we were within the weight limit. When the pilot asked if anyone in our party wanted to ride up front in the co-pilot seat, Steve raised his hand.

"I actually took an aviation class in high school and flew a Cessna as part of it," Steve said.

The pilot laughed and replied, "Well, that makes you more qualified than anyone else here, I suppose, so jump on in."

Of course, we all knew if something catastrophic actually did happen to the pilot, we were all likely to die in a fiery crash, or perhaps even drown in one of the many lakes. So, instead of being reassured at the savvy of my friend despite his high school aeronautical muscle-flex, I said a prayer for a safe flight.

Prior to loading our gear, they boarded a couple of fifty-five-gallon drums of diesel fuel into the Otter's cargo hold. Steve and I looked at each other surprised. I suppose they needed to get fuel to the generators at Uchi Lodge somehow, but I just didn't think I'd be riding next to one in coach. My initial thought about a fiery crash took on a new significance knowing I could serve as human barbeque in the event of a pilot heart attack.

We were all given earplugs for the flight, yet another first in all my years of air travel. I soon found out why as the pilot fired up the engine and we began taxiing toward our takeoff path. Even with the earplugs in, the noise was intense. It was only squelched by my excitement at taking off from water to sky. The powerful engine cackled and buzzed like a World War II Spitfire. We turned and taxied slowly until the pilot was happy with his course. Then, he hit the throttle and the sound became deafening, even with earplugs, louder and louder until we were finally airborne. It was an adrenaline boosting lift-off from the lake.

Once we were airborne at cruising altitude, a couple of things became glaringly apparent. First, Ontario is largely a vast wilderness with thousands of lakes and millions of acres of forest. It was endless in all directions with only the occasional highway bisecting the forest or the periodic resort dotting the landscape.

The other striking feature from above were the scars of cleared land where large areas of forest were cut by loggers. Normally I would have been saddened by the sight of these broad swaths of destruction, but after seeing so much woodland from above, I began to understand the idea that the lumber and pulp industry had a legitimate place in these remote areas. There was virtually an unlimited supply. Later in the week, I would find out from one of the guides at the resort that these logged areas are replanted, as required by law. In fact, Canada has some of the most rigorous forest management laws of anywhere in the world. While I realize that the monoculture of these mass plantings in no way replicates the biodiversity of the forest they were destroying, at least it was *something*. Knowing this was a great relief to my inner environmentalist after seeing the scabbed areas of this beautiful wilderness.

* * *

Once we landed and unloaded our gear, we checked in with Judy, the resort owner who pointed us to our unit. The cabin accommodations were small but adequate. Our place had two bedrooms, a small living area and a kitchen sink off to one side. It was rudimentary and sparse but suited us well. Perhaps the biggest blessing was the lack of a television. It meant we would have to spend our time conversing and getting to know one another better. Besides, I hated television at home, let alone in the great north country of Canada.

We were both anxious to get as much time on the water as we could during our three days, so after we unpacked, we headed out fishing. The result was a tough day on the water, particularly for me. Steve managed to get a couple of northern pike, but I struggled mightily. I was frustrated, especially given all the Canadian fishing stories leading up to the trip. I'd heard of catching so many fish you actually got tired of it. It appeared there would be none of that happening on this particular day. Frankly, I would have sold a little piece of my soul for just a taste of it. I chalked it up to learning a new lake and hoped we'd have a chance for redemption during our evening outing.

Dinner was held in the common-area dining room of Uchi Lake Lodge. It was a large open area overlooking the lake and featured a number of tables spread around including a small separate area for lounging before or after meals.

At dinner we shared our struggles of the afternoon to a couple of the guests. One of them had mentioned a possible spot to try east of the resort and showed us roughly where it was on the map. When we finished dinner, Steve and I headed out to see if we could redeem our struggles of earlier in the day. We were looking for any kind of a break, so boarded our boat and motored our way toward the alleged hot spot.

At the location, we baited our jigs with minnows and dropped them over the side. Jigging minnows off the bottom of the lake wasn't a technique I'd done a lot of, but it seemed fairly straightforward. Drop it down, let it hit and every few seconds, lift it a little to entice the walleye.

The tricky part to walleye fishing is the hookset. It is a very different technique than the immediate, spastic rod jerks conducted when you get a bite while casting. It requires a unique form of patience. As you're jigging, you feel a little tug on your line which, contrary to instinct, means you wait a few more seconds before you set the hook. If you don't wait to ensure the fish has it, you will likely lose it. Trust me, I've lost more than my share, in large part due to a lack of patience. It is all about timing.

The evening was clear and warm as the sun hung low on the horizon. The water was calm and there was a slight breeze from the west, enough to push the boat at a slow drift. This natural drift would allow us to cover a little more ground in case the fish were moving.

Within five minutes of Steve killing the motor, I had a nibble. I waited a few seconds and then set the hook.

"Got one!"

"Really? Nice!" Steve said, happy one of us had a fish.

I pulled up a nice little thirteen-incher and lifted it into the boat. A couple of minutes later, Steve said, "Oh, I think I felt something too. I might have one here."

"Yeah? Bring him in!"

Steve set the hook and brought in another walleye. Before he could get it off the hook, I had another one on.

"Hey, dude, I got another one. I think we're on 'em here," I said.

"Seems like it!"

A couple of fish later, the bite went cold. Evidently, we'd drifted into deeper water and off of the fish.

"I think we're too deep. What I am going to do, Jim, is motor us back over there where we started catching them and we'll run this drift line again," Steve said.

"Sounds like a plan. That was a fun little stretch there."

Steve pulled the ripcord and we motored back twenty yards to where we'd started. When we began our second drift, we both visually marked our location. Fish are often territorial, and we wanted to remember where we were, not only for tonight's effort, but for tomorrow and the next day as well. As we drifted this second time, my ratio of fish to Steve's was about 3:1. I made the rookie mistake of saying, "I think I've caught like eight to your two, Steve."

"Oh, what? You're counting now?" Steve replied.

"Oops! I meant that as a team we have ten fish."

"That's better, but it's not what I heard the first time."

I laughed at my own prideful and selfish declaration. In all my excitement I'd forgotten how much it sucked when someone else was catching more fish than me. How quickly the tide had turned, and me along with it.

Steve's success shortly matched my own. We were catching three to four fish virtually every drift. Eventually the minnow supply began to dwindle. The thought of motoring back to camp for more meant we'd lose valuable fishing time. This far north it stayed light until 9:30 in mid-summer, but our time in the twilight was beginning to make it difficult to see. Eventually we ran out of live minnows and began using dead ones from the bottom of the boat. The funny thing was, they actually worked! By the time we'd used all of the dead cast-offs, we decided to call it a night.

I will always remember those hours at dusk as the best night of fishing, ever. We probably caught 30-40 fish between us over two and a half hours. There were times when we both had one on the line simultaneously, a phenomenon known as a doubleheader. It was my first real exposure to nonstop action and restored my faith in the tales I'd heard of Canadian fishing, of catching so many you get tired of it. While that feeling had not stricken me yet, the night had proven to me that it could happen.

But perhaps more importantly, the night broke our friendship wide open. The frustration of the afternoon's struggles gave way to a bountiful catch in the fading light of the Ontario wilderness. In a sense, relationally, we had cast the net over to the other side of the boat, to reference a biblical metaphor. Our mutual success accompanied by playful banter had managed to eliminate any remaining awkwardness between us. That night moved us from friends to lifelong friends.

Since then, Steve and I have fished together for hundreds of hours and caught amazing fish of all species. In the process we have come to refer to one another as brother on occasion and built enough memories to support the reference. It has become a friendship or brotherhood forged by an evening of camaraderie in the fading corona of a Canadian sunset.

* * *

After our success that night, I was really looking forward to a good night's sleep. I hadn't slept more than a few hours each of the previous two days. The night before we left on the trip was a restless one, my mind busy with details and whether I'd packed everything I needed. The next night, during our stay in the hotel in Sioux Lookout, I was kept awake by Steve's snoring. I am a man who needs his eight hours, so my two-night sleep deprivation was beginning to take its toll.

When we docked the boat and got back to the cabin, we stayed up for a bit to unwind after our day. We had a few beers and made a couple trips each to the shared bathroom a short walk from our cabin. These trips outdoors brought to light that the mosquitoes in Canada were a level above anything I'd ever experienced, even as a lifelong Midwesterner. They were big, thirsty and plentiful.

After washing up for the evening, we said our goodnights and went to our respective bedrooms. Within five minutes I heard the telltale buzz of a mosquito near my face.

Frankly, nothing obsesses me more than a bloodsucking insect flying around my room as I lay there as a defenseless human target. I've spent enough nights in a tent with a few stray mosquitoes and there is nothing fun about it. The buzz alone is annoying and is only made worse when it stops, and the guessing game begins. Where is it? Did it land? Is it on my face?

My fears were answered soon enough when the noise stopped. I shut my eyes and tried not to think about it. Thirty seconds later, I heard it buzzing again. I swatted furiously in its direction and pulled the covers up even more. It was then I heard Steve's snoring, buzzing like a giant human mosquito, through the thin walls of the cabin. Oh, no. Here we go. Another sleepless night, I thought. It was pretty clear I was perilously situated on the threshold of hell. If not, I could certainly see it from there.

In a state of abject frustration, I got up, turned on the light and hunted a couple of the mosquitoes down. One I managed to smash left a blood streak on the cabin wall. If I was to wager a guess, it was probably my blood, A-positive and recently withdrawn from my veins. The visual evidence only fueled my overactive obsession about these godforsaken insects disrupting my sleep.

Content I'd succeeded in eradicating the problem, I turned off the light and tried to get back to sleep. Ten minutes later, I heard it again. The buzz of this one changed the focus of my attention from Steve's snoring back to the thought of another itchy welt. The combination of auditory distractions had me in the grips of my own personal Tell-Tale Heart. Nobody else could hear it, and it was slowly driving me to the brink of madness!

I threw back the covers and got up again to switch on the light, my obsession raging at full roar. *Where were they coming from? Were they breeding in here?* I looked around the room and realized there was a small gap between my door and the frame. *Maybe they're coming through those gaps!* I may not have been thinking 100% rationally at this point.

I grabbed my towel, rolled it up and tucked it in at the base of the door. I closed a t-shirt in the door at the widest gap near the top, just to make sure there were no possible points-of-entry from our living room. Then, I went through my suitcase and found my mosquito jacket, essentially a hooded jacket made entirely out of mosquito netting. I put it on and cinched the hood over my head and face. To most people this might seem excessive, but to my sleep-deprived brain, it seemed totally logical.

I did one last scan of the room and shut out the light. I laid down in the comfort of knowing at least my head would no longer be a feasible target and I'd be able to get some rest. I closed my eyes and heard, buzz, snore, buzz, snore.

Threshold of hell, I say!

* * *

The next morning, I heard Steve knock and say, "Hey, Jim. What is this tucked in your door?" I rose and opened the door. I stood there in my mosquito jacket and pajama bottoms. Steve looked at me and cracked up.

"What are you doing?"

"I slept in this, that's what I'm doing. I have what you might call a bug problem," I replied.

Steve couldn't stop laughing. His compassion took a back seat to the entertainment value of his fishing partner who'd just slept in a mosquito jacket.

"Ha, ha! I can't believe you slept in that."

"Well, I wouldn't really call it sleeping. It was more like moments of light napping strung loosely together. Judging from the volume of your snoring, I know you slept well."

"Oh, did I snore again? Sorry about that. I'll give you some earplugs for tonight," he said.

"Thanks. If I don't sleep good soon, I'm gonna die," I said.

We went about our day and were much more careful with the cabin door that night. We'd been careless once and it was the source of the infestation, a mistake we didn't want to repeat. At bedtime, I conducted a thorough bug search before turning in. The last thing I remember was putting in my earplugs and drifting off to the first full night of sleep in four days.

* * *

The rest of our fly-in trip at Uchi Lake was filled with fish, laughter, comradery, and shore lunches. In all honesty, leading up to the trip I didn't know what to expect from a friendship standpoint. In the end, it turned out to be a great thing for a couple of guys whose wives were best friends. The interactions and resultant memories from the trip raised our friendship to the next level. Our teamwork in the boat, the drive-time conversations, and all of the laughs in between, helped us realize our commonalities were worth investing in. I am forever grateful for that trip and the fallout of it, namely a longstanding friendship with Steve.

Niobe Lake

Out on the reef
the walleyes come in to feed
innocently.

After our success at Uchi Lake and a highly positive experience with Canadian fishing, Steve and I committed to making a return a couple of years later. Our wives were fully supportive provided they were granted their own girlfriend vacations somewhere to even the score. Steve also thought it might be fun to have a third person on the trip, so he talked to our friend Dave to see if he would be interested. Dave was a guy I'd met a few times before who seemed like a perfect fit. He wasn't as seasoned a fisherman as Steve and I but had a huge heart and a great sense of humor. He said he'd love to join us.

We decided to change things up a little for this second venture into Canada. While we enjoyed the Uchi Lake fly-in, we thought we could save a little money by doing a drive-in trip to one of the many resorts in Ontario. In preparation, we attended the All-Canada show in Milwaukee in January of 2008 to get a feel for our options. There is nothing that gets a fisherperson more excited in the dead of winter than attending a show like this. The exhibit hall was packed with tables and displays representing all parts of Canada with over a hundred vendors hawking their resorts. It was the equivalent to an outdoor lover's Comic-Con.

The three of us arrived at the exhibit hall on the evening it opened. After stopping for a Labatt Blue beer, we started strolling aisle-by-aisle through the various vendor tables. About halfway through our evening we ended up talking at length to Marty and Deb, a husband-and-wife team who ran Niobe Lake Lodge. As we talked about amenities and prices, one of the other gentlemen standing by the table said, "You guys will *not* be disappointed if you book with these folks. They will get you on the fish and are great hosts!"

It's strange how a recommendation like that has an effect on people. I'm sure, had we tried hard enough, we could have gotten testimonials from people for any one of the vendors at the show. One really can't go wrong with Canadian fishing, but for some reason this guy's comments resonated. After a little more discussion with Marty and Deb, we continued on our way down the aisle.

"That place sounds really good. They said the guide would take you to fish whatever species you wanted," I said.

"Yeah, and that guy standing there sure had good things to say," Steve replied.

"We may have found our place," I said.

"Sounded good to me," Dave added.

We continued on our way around the arena, but after Niobe, all the other places sounded second-rate. Whether it was price, distance, or offerings, none of the others seemed as appealing as Niobe. We left the arena all jittery with excitement for the coming summer, despite being stuck in the frigid cold of a January night. Clouds of breath hung in the air as we talked on the way to our cars. When we separated, I sang out, "Oh, Canada!" The guys laughed and continued on their way. The pending hope of walleye shore lunches and long Canadian summer days had taken me away. Within a couple weeks of the show, we booked a trip with them for four days and five nights in June of 2008. I could hardly wait.

*   *   *

After a grueling twelve-hour drive, the three of us arrived at Niobe Lake Lodge, just outside of Atikokan, Ontario. We checked in with Marty and Deb. They were warm and welcoming and felt more like family than business owners. They made it clear from the outset it was their job to see to it that we caught fish and were well-fed. We'd purchased the guided American plan which included all meals, fish cleaning and housekeeping for the cabin. This plan cost a little more, but we'd decided early on we wanted this to be a vacation from *everything*, not a working vacation. None of us was interested in cooking meals, housework or cleaning fish. So, the American plan it was.

Once our cabin was pointed out to us, we unpacked the SUV and got situated. It was clear these units were a step above the accommodations offered at Uchi Lake, in large part because everything didn't need to be flown in by float plane. I was a little surprised and, frankly, disappointed to see they were all equipped with small TVs hooked up to satellite dishes. I am one who likes to escape all conveniences when I go on vacation, especially television. But it was what it was.

When dinner was finished, we were all a little anxious to get some fishing in. Our guided time didn't officially start until the next morning, but Marty said a boat was available any time in the event that we wanted to try our luck on Niobe Lake.

We took him up on his offer and piled our gear into the boat. Steve took the motor spot while Dave and I sat in the middle and bow seats. We motored out a short way before the bantering and boasting started.

"First fish gets five bucks from the other two guys," I said.

"It's on!" Dave replied.

It is a well-known fact these bets are never paid. They serve as a motivational challenge, but we all know we'll never see any money exchanged. It's just part of the fun.

With the stakes defined, we began casting with fury. We knew nothing of the lake, and it showed. It was an hour before Dave finally said, "I think I got one here!"

"Really? Nice," Steve replied.

Dave reeled in a medium-sized northern pike. It was nothing to write home about, but it was a fish, and that was to be celebrated by all.

"Look at that, fellas. First fish of the week, baby!" Dave boasted.

"Nice going. Let's hope it's a sign of things to come," I replied.

"I hear that," Steve added.

We hadn't really expected much on this first night, so this fish was a bonus. This was a new resort with lots of unknowns. How would the fishing be? Will a guide be worth the extra cost? How will Dave do with four straight days of fishing? These questions would all be answered over the next four days, but the fish he'd caught had us all excited. We could barely contain our excitement at getting out the next morning and hitting it hard. Leave it to the new guy to get the fire stoked. We spent another half hour in futility before we gave up and motored home.

* * *

In the morning, we met our guide at about 7:30. He was a few years older than us with a three-day beard and that rugged look of a fishing guide who'd spent many long days under a Canadian sun. He said the arrangement would be that he would run one of the boats with one of us, and Steve would run the second with the other guy. The order would change every day or two to ensure everyone got a chance to maximize their time actually fishing and not worrying about the path of the boat.

Because the days all tended to look the same, the exact chronology of all the fish we caught escapes me. I do have a few memorable moments the three of us still recall with fondness and laughter.

The first of these occurred one day when I was in the boat with our guide, Mike. It was one of the rare occasions where I was catching fish and he was not. After the third walleye in a row to Mike's zero, I managed to snag my jig on the bottom of the lake. I pulled and yanked with determination, all to no avail. Mike watched me struggle for about three minutes before he took out his pocketknife and cut my line. Then he turned to the other boat and said, "Reel 'em up. We're moving!"

I stood there with my broken line stifling my laugh at the abruptness and certainty of his decision. It seemed a bit discourteous, at least from the perspective of a paying customer. Typically, guides are self-sacrificing when it comes to their clients. I once had a guide on Lake Mille Lacs in Minnesota exchange rods with me when my line was snagged. He then went about trying to free it while I fished with his. If the line he was trying to recover broke, he would set it up and hand it back to me. After that treatment worthy of royalty, I assumed it was the way it was done by *all* guides.

But this was different. To add to the line-cutting, Mike's decision to move elsewhere, despite the fact I'd been catching fish and, well, it was all just funny to me. I didn't harbor any resentment against him, but I sure got a laugh from the boys when I told the story back at the cabin that night. We all thought it seemed a little brusque.

Another memorable incident, and I might even call it a teachable moment, happened on another day when I was in the boat with Mike. Dave managed to hook into a nice northern pike and when he finally landed it, he started hooting and hollering. After about the third time, Mike shouted over to him to quiet down. That kind of shouting attracted the attention of other people fishing around us and tipped them off as to our location. Mike knew the lake like the back of his hand, so giving any clues to where the hot spots were was discouraged. Furthermore, he had clients all summer long, so giving away his favorite spots was not a good business model.

Dave apologized. I can't blame him for getting excited about such a beautiful fish, probably the biggest he'd ever caught. Fishing sometimes leads to uncontrolled outbursts. At the same time, I totally understood Mike's point. I am a fairly quiet person, normally. When it comes to fishing, I take it up a notch. In my case, it is more a concern for not scaring the fish than it is about attracting undue attention to a location. Fishing for me is meditative and best done in hushed tones. Even when I caught my big Muskies, I've kept my celebrations to the people in the boat. Everyone is different though, and as I said, this was a teachable moment for all of us. Good fishing spots are hard to find and should be shared only with close friends.

Another memorable incident happened after a long day of fishing. We told Mike we needed to stop in town on the way home to get some beer and cigars. We'd run out of both and still had a couple days left in Ontario. Mike said that was fine and he'd meet us back at the lodge.

We stopped in a liquor store in Atikokan and walked in. The inside looked like any American liquor store as we strolled among the selection. However, we were shocked to see a case of Labatt Blue beer cost forty-two US dollars! Labatt Blue is equivalent to Miller High Life in the US. There is nothing special about either of these beers.

Steve and Dave both looked at me with identical looks of disbelief.

I said in a low voice, dripping with sarcasm, "Well it is Labatt's, after all."

"Yeah, there is that," Steve said with a laugh.

"Well, there really is no alternative, is there? This is as cheap as it comes. It only goes up from here," I said.

"As much as it hurts, we gotta do it, guys," Dave added.

We picked up a case and approached the counter. Dave asked for a pack of cigars as well. He and I had both run out of the few we had brought. The pack the clerk sold us caused similar sticker shock to both of us. We deduced that either Canadians were paying a lot for their vices, or else we were being fleeced as American tourists. I'm still not sure which was true.

On top of these moments of levity and laughter, my time fishing in Canada at Niobe Lake Lodge comprised some of the best fishing I'd ever experienced. The trip continues to hold my personal bests in three different species (walleye, 29.5", bass, 19.5", and northern pike 36"). We'd all had great success that first year in 2008. So much so, when the time came to leave, we chipped in $100.00 each to offer as a tip to Mike. We approached him after he'd cleaned our last fish and was ready to head home.

"Hey Mike, we just wanted to say how much we appreciate your guiding us and consistently getting us on fish. Here's a little something for you," Steve said.

He handed Mike the three one-hundred-dollar bills. Mike was caught off guard.

"Wow! You guys need to come fishing with me more often," he said.

We laughed and thanked him again. We tipped the same, two years later when we went up to Niobe again. He was a great guide and always took us where the fish were.

Those years at Niobe were great fun and second-to-none from a fishing standpoint. By day four, we were almost sick of catching walleye, and, believe me, I never thought I'd say something like that. In many respects, those trips spoiled me as a fisherman. I knew I could never match it back in the states. It is for these reasons that talk of returning to Ontario has begun again. This time however, it involves a location that includes the mighty Muskellunge.

It is also the reason I occasionally send Dave and Steve a random two-word text reading, "Oh, Canada!"

Birch Lake

Minnow on a hook
little fish catches big fish
law of the water.

As time went on, Steve and I have fished bass and walleye a number of times in Wisconsin and Canada. We always got along great in the boat, with plenty of verbal jousting and chiding along with side-splitting laughter. For a few years he tried to convince me to go up north in October for Muskie fishing. He'd shown me pictures of trophy fish he and others caught in prior years while staying at a friend's cabin near Presque Isle, Wisconsin.

While I was intrigued by the possibility of catching the biggest fish of my life, I was equally deterred by the other things that were part of Steve's description of the process. For starters, in all the pictures he showed me, he was wearing a winter coat, hat and gloves. It just looked damn cold! One of my arguments against the idea was, I was a fair-weather fisherman. The thought of having to wear a winter coat while in a boat in late fall just didn't appeal to me.

The second red flag in his sales pitch was the mention that it involved row-trolling. Because motorized trolling was illegal at the time, he said one person typically rowed the boat while the other cast out the front. Now, I am as in-shape as the next guy, but it just sounded like a whole lot of work. Combined that with the fact you'd be rowing in a winter jacket and, well, you could count me out.

The final straw though, was his reminder that for the first four years he went, he never caught a Muskie. Other guys he fished with did, but Steve hadn't. I recalled what my brother Tom said years prior, "Jim, when I go fishing, I like to actually catch something." That was my take on it as well. Combined with the other two previously mentioned variables, the appeal of fall Muskie fishing just didn't shake my tree.

In any case, after about three years of Steve asking, I finally relented and said I'd go. I was spurred in part by my desire to get my first Muskie and get the monkey off my back. Two of my brothers had caught Muskies and I really wanted to find out what the big deal was. Besides, unless I tried it to see how I liked it, I would never know. At the same time, if I decided I didn't like it, I could always say no the next year.

Steve explained he typically stayed with his friend John, who had a cabin near Presque Isle. It was a small, but modern two-bedroom place in the woods with a pullout futon couch. The thought of a free place to stay, a couple days of fishing and a few adult beverages with friends, sounded too good to pass up. I would have to see for myself if all the apparent hardships were worth it.

Steve was a teacher for Milwaukee Public Schools and worked on what was known as a year-round schedule. Instead of a three-month summer break, the schedule had a few two-week breaks every couple of months over the school year. As it worked out, one of his breaks conveniently fell in mid-October when Muskie fishing was just beginning to heat up. We set a date for a long weekend and cleared it with John. We would drive up on Thursday night after work, fish Friday and Saturday and come home on Sunday.

Now, if you're like me, so much of a vacation is about the journey. I positively relish a good road trip. I love the hum of the road, the changing scenery, the anticipation of getting there and all the rest. What I like best though, is the time it gives me to think and reflect on life. My brain percolates on the present; how things are going. The miles allow for looks back at my past and provide recognition of how blessed I am to have all I have. The road is hypnotic and thought-provoking. It helps channel my inner Buddha.

As it turned out, Steve and I were great traveling companions. We shared similar musical tastes, we both loved to drive, and both respected the need for naps or quiet time as needed. When our wives have traveled together in the past, they have said how great it felt to be able to talk uninterrupted for five hours. They've asked us what we talk about on our trips and found it hilarious when we told them we can go for an hour at a time without saying a word. It's not that we don't have things to talk about, but we both like listening to music, thinking and just being quiet. We usually passed a bag of Twizzlers licorice between us for thirty or forty miles just to pass the time. When we discovered our mutual love for the candy, we knew we'd probably be good traveling partners. We sit and chew our strawberry licorice cuds like a couple of nine-year-olds while the miles roll by. It's a sugar-fueled mental health session.

Steve picked me up at five p.m. and we headed west on I-94. Nearly four hours later, we came to an iconic underpass that had come to signal our arrival up north every year. It was an old iron railroad bridge some high-schoolers had tagged with graffiti years earlier. Emblazoned in four-foot tall letters in plain view of any northbound vehicle were the words, T-BIRD COUNTRY. The local school mascot was the Thunderbird, so these students thought it was important to declare their boundary using paint and a little dash of risk. Since Highway 51 was a main thoroughfare for people going north for vacation, the bridge and its slogan became a notable landmark for years. It was finally taken down and a new one constructed in 2018. Progress evidently has no care for nostalgia. In any case, the excitement always grew when we passed under the T-Bird bridge on the outskirts of Hazelhurst.

We pulled into Manitowish Waters at about nine-thirty p.m. The town held another notable point of interest for Steve from his past trips up Muskie fishing. It was home to the Pea Patch Motel and Saloon, a landmark watering hole in the great northwoods.

"Yeah, I figure we'll stop at the Pea Patch for a beer on the way in. Kind of a tradition," Steve said.

"Hey, you don't have to ask me twice," I replied with a laugh.

Steve pulled into the lot lined with half a dozen other vehicles. When we walked in most of the patrons turned and gawked, a common practice in most bars north of Wausau when anyone new entered. Of course, no one recognized us, except the bartender who remembered Steve from years past. The rest of the regulars were hunched over their Miller Lites or brandy old fashioneds. Most of the men wore ball caps and some combination of flannel and jeans, the uniform of a Wisconsin outdoorsman. It was apparent right away we were city boys and no harm or threat, so everyone went back to their drinks and conversations and left us to ourselves.

The Pea Patch Motel has a series of rooms for rent adjacent to the bar. The establishment is situated next to the Rest Lake dam on the Manitowish chain of lakes. The sign out front plays on this location by using the catchy slogan, "The best burger by a dam site." Inside, the long wooden bar has historic photos of the original building as well as some old black and white shots of trophy Muskies and area landmarks forever immortalized under a layer of lacquer. A series of TVs hung from the wall broadcasting various football games.

We both ordered beers and found a table near the fully occupied bar. Steve and I talked about our strategy for fishing the next couple of days. John had to work, so wouldn't be up until Friday evening. He had given Steve instructions on where everything was for his boat, trailer and Muskie rods. I was flummoxed with the level of John's generosity and trust with every important possession of his recreational life. I'd never met him, I already knew I'd like him. Anyone that selfless was okay in my book. After we drained our beers, we climbed back into Steve's SUV and finished out the last 25 minutes of our trip.

* * *

John's cabin was a newly constructed place in a wooded area set off from the main county highway. There was no lake frontage, but as John said, his place is within thirty minutes of a few dozen "Class A" Muskie lakes. Lake frontage in the area is expensive and comes with a much higher tax bill. This cabin was centrally located to get him in the thick of the game, to say nothing of all the other species and additional outdoor sporting opportunities.

As we walked in, the cabin was quaint and homey with lots of tasteful up-north decorating touches. My favorite was a hand-carved sculpture of a Muskie chasing a bait fish that was hanging on the living room wall. It was a beautifully stained wooden representation of everything we were up there for, and a nice divergence from the taxidermy mounts so commonly seen up north.

A large wood-burning stove sat off the main living area and served as a cheap source of heat to augment the electric baseboards throughout the place. The living space was open concept, all one level with the kitchen, dining and living areas all easily accessible. Double-paned windows and well insulated walls meant the place heated up quickly and could be used year-round. Off to one side of the cabin sat a double garage for stowing John's boat, kayaks, various tools and lawn equipment. In my eyes, the entire property was an absolutely perfect setup for a Northwoods getaway. After unpacking the car, Steve and I chatted and had a couple of nightcap beers before bed.

* * *

We woke up Friday morning at about seven o'clock and started our day. Temps were in the low forties with the forecast for mid-fifties and partly cloudy skies in the afternoon. Not a bad forecast for that part of the state at that time of the year, at all. This area of the state can get threats of lake-effect snow as early as Late August with annual totals nearing 100 inches or more. I'll take mid-fifties in October any day of the week.

I scarfed down a banana and a granola bar, then washed it down with a cup of coffee from John's Keurig coffee maker. Steve is not a breakfast guy when it comes to early morning fishing, preferring to snack on the boat later in the day. So, he packed while I scarfed.

We hitched John's boat and trailer to Steve's SUV, plugged in the lights and loaded up the car. The standard boat equipment included two trolling rods, two casting rods, tackle boxes, a snack and beverage cooler, rain gear and a dry bag used to keep phones, keys and wallets from getting wet. When prepping for a full day on a boat, packing well is imperative.

On the way to the lake, we stopped at a gas station with a sign out front that read, "Welcome Muskie Fishermen! Suckers, Ice, Beer." Not knowing the drill, I followed Steve into the store.

"How you doin' today? Can we get four suckers when you get a chance?" Steve asked the attendant.

"Sure thing," the clerk replied. She picked up a phone and passed his request on to another attendant somewhere out back.

"I got these," I told Steve. I wanted to pull my weight financially on this trip to be sure I was welcomed back in case I wanted to come the following year. No one likes a skinflint traveling companion.

When she rang up the total of $24.00 for the four baits, I almost coughed up my granola bar from sticker shock. Six bucks a piece for baits? I thought, Holy cripes! After I saw how big they were and heard how they could be difficult to come by some years, I understood. But still. It was becoming increasingly clear to me, that Muskie fishing was different from your run-of-the-mill pursuit of walleye and bass.

We dumped the suckers and a generous amount of water into the live well and shut the lid. The well had an automated water intake which would allow us to add additional fresh lake water after launching. If the well water was kept fresh and periodically changed, the suckers would last the whole weekend. Of course, it was our hope that they'd serve as lunch for a Muskie instead. I'd pay $6.00 each all day long if we were catching fish. But we had to plan for a worst-case scenario and try and keep them alive. Heck, at that price, I'd give them mouth-to-mouth resuscitation if they needed it.

After a fifteen-minute drive to the lake, we launched. Steve motored out a bit and then killed the engine. The trees along the shore were burning with post-peak autumn color creating a breathtaking vista in the cool of this fall morning. Brown, gold and amber trees rimmed the lake as they held their leaves for another day before eventually falling in a nod to the coming winter.

I watched as Steve patiently set up the suckers with quick-strike rigs. These rigs consist of a pair of treble hooks and a wire harness intended to insure a hookset was successful and the fish was released healthy after a catch. Setting up the suckers on the rigs was an intricate process and yet another reminder of the unique qualities of fishing this species. It was clear to me this was more like hunting, than fishing. Big fish required lots of prep and specialized equipment.

I powered up the depth finder and Steve began to instruct me on how things worked.

"Okay, Jim, now what you're going to want to do is row us along the shoreline but keep us between eight and ten feet of water. I'll keep an eye on the suckers and maybe cast a little if I get a chance. When you get tired, let me know and we can switch. I've found that rowing is a good way to keep yourself warm."

I moved to the middle seat and grabbed the oars. At the time, Wisconsin had a no motor-trolling law, so rowing was the only legal way to troll for Muskie. It still seemed like such a primitive way to fish; especially given we had a perfectly good trolling motor bolted to the bow. Of course, having a brother who served as the DNR Commissioner a state away in Minnesota, I wasn't about to break the law and risk an embarrassing headline in the newspaper. But still, the law seemed excessive and trite. (This law was abolished several years later.)

I rowed us out to a nine-foot depth and tried to keep us there while maintaining a slow troll. Steve moved to the front and started casting. It was a beautiful autumn day with high clouds, no wind, and a glass-like finish to the water. We were both dressed warmly and, I had to admit, it was great to be outdoors fishing. On an ordinary year, my fishing typically ended at the Labor Day holiday. This was like a bonus outing.

After an hour and a half, we switched places. I moved to the front of the boat and took my first shot at using Steve's rod and baitcast reel. I knew they were tricky devices, as I recalled Rob's struggles during his first experience with one at Spider Lake years earlier. Steve filled me in on the details of how to cast. I listened, but apparently did not hear. I kept my thumb on the spool, reared back and let it sail. The lure splashed down and the spool instantly erupted into a tangled mess. It went about as badly as I could have expected and, like most rookies, I got my first bird's nest on the first cast. "Oh, man, what happened?" I asked, bewildered.

"Did you keep your thumb on the spool and then stop it once the lure hit the water?" Steve asked.

"Ummm, maybe I didn't do that, no," I confessed.

"Awww, dude…" Steve laughed.

I spent the next twenty minutes trying to undo the mess. I felt bad because it was Steve's rod and reel, and I didn't want to ruin a good day of fishing this early in the trip.

Eventually, I got the tangle undone and went back to casting. The subsequent attempts were much better as Steve continued coaching me on the nuances of using a baitcaster. By the end of the day, I was casting with a decent level of confidence and precision. If there's one thing I hate as a fisherman, it's unnecessary downtime, so I was determined to get it right!

Every good Muskie fisherman finishes his lure retrieval with what's known as a figure-eight. It is a technique where you put the rod deep into the water and draw a figure-eight. The fish sometimes follow a lure for the entire retrieve, and often strike at this point if a figure-eight is conducted correctly. Despite his attempts to teach me the technique, I struggled the whole day learning it. Mine were more like figure-sixes. There might even have been a "niner" in there. I felt more like a little kid goofing around over the side of the boat than doing anything that might prove attractive to a fish. I was pretty sure it was only serving to drive away any that might have followed anyway. I kept at it nonetheless and tried to at least appear I was putting forth an effort.

We fished the entire morning and afternoon with nothing but a few false alarm snags on the suckers we were trolling. At about 3:30 we took a well-deserved break. I stopped rowing and we enjoyed a couple of ham sandwiches and beers from the cooler. After my sandwich, I lit a cigar, kicked my feet up and just relaxed for a bit. Around that time, we heard the telltale tick-tick-tick of the drag from one of the sucker reels. We watched as the bobber started to move away from the boat. "That's a fish on there, Jim. Start working us back toward the bobber," Steve said.

We were both excited something was finally happening. I grabbed the oars and maneuvered the boat toward the bobber. Every time I approached it, it started moving away from us again. We kept hoping for the bobber to fall off as it was designed to, but it never did. After a couple minutes of chasing it, Steve said I was just going to have to set the hook with the bobber on. At this point, I was so antsy to get the fish into the boat the bobber was the least of my worries.

Steve then looked over at me and said, "On three, set the hook, okay? And set it with force!"

"Yep, will do," I replied.

As I counted to three, I reeled up the line slack all the way to the water line, then reared back and set the hook with intent and purpose. The fish fought hard and dove away. When it ran, I held on. Then when it slacked, I began reeling frantically. After twenty seconds or so, she was boat side, and Steve scooped her into the giant net.

I had done it! I'd bagged my first Muskie! I was shaking from head to toe with excitement and adrenaline, knowing I'd achieved something many fishermen never would. It was an amazing feeling, almost as though my entire fishing career had come to its zenith. Furthermore, the monkey was finally off my back, and everything it took to get here was worth it.

Steve lifted the fish into the boat. It measured in at thirty-six inches, small as Muskies go, but still a respectable fish for a first timer. With its vertical stripes and long powerful body, it was a thing of beauty. It had a decent sized gash on its back, perhaps from a battle with another fish some time ago. We snapped a couple of pictures and then set her free. She swam away into the copper-colored water with a nice sucker in her gut for her trouble.

After the dust cleared and I had time to think about it, I realized this outing got me unequivocally hooked. I now understood the purpose behind spending hours or sometimes days in search of a Muskie. I finally saw what Paul and Rob were talking about when they said there's nothing like the feeling. These are not like your everyday bass or walleye. Our buddy John always says, "as freshwater fish go, they're top of the food chain." To catch them you need patience, dedication and a lot of stamina. All my trepidations about the weather and other hardships were quickly laid to rest. And while it's not a sport for everyone, I am a good example of a complete and total convert. I also realize, that like any good hunt, the waiting is half the fun.

* * *

Because of my newfound zeal for the sport, Steve and I made it a point to get up to John's place every fall in search of these magnificent fish. Over the years, one of the things I've come to look forward to on our visits is our stops at a bar called the Retreat. The bar is a very short distance from John's place and makes a nice diversion from the confines of the cabin. More importantly, it provides a little social interaction and all the accompanying adult silliness.

The bar itself is U-shaped, the open end at the top providing access for the bartender to restock the liquor and grab the food orders from the small kitchen out back. It also allows easy conversation across to the other side of the bar if the need presents itself. There are a few slot machines flashing their attraction near the table seating area. At any given time of day, the dice cup can be heard slamming against the bar top in a battle for dollar bills between friends.

When we first started going up there the bar was owned and operated by Gary. He was a cool, yet sometimes cantankerous dude with a ZZ Top-length beard and a set of the most bowed legs I'd ever seen. Steve once quipped about how they looked like they could snap at any moment because they were under such pressure given the arc angles they held. He was a great bartender though and an up-north fixture whose passing was mourned by the whole community.

After his death the Retreat was purchased by new owners, Beth and Jim. Because John was a regular at the place, Steve and I, who only get up there once a year, always got a, "they're with me" pass with folks like Beth and Jim. John is well-known and liked up there, making us good guys via association. It doesn't hurt our level of service either.

In 2010, I looked forward to my second year of Muskie fishing. Steve and I met John around eight o'clock at the Pea Patch and had a couple beers. Steve ordered a Bud Light and I, being a beer connoisseur, ordered an India Pale Ale, which turned out to be one of the less informed decisions I've ever made up north. If you know IPAs, you know they are hoppy and strong. To add to the situation, Steve is a fast drinker. Of course, not wanting to lag behind on buying rounds I tried to keep pace with my IPAs to his Bud Lights.

After a couple of drinks, we decided to change venues down the road to the Retreat. So, we piled into the car and headed east. By the time we got there, I was feeling good. We were up north, the beer was flowing, and a day of fishing for the most sought-after fish in the state lay ahead of us.

We ordered another round and played a little bar dice. As often happens in situations where everyone is on vacation and feeling good, our judgment began to stray from the highway of common sense.

"How about a shot, boys?" John said.

Now, I hadn't drank like this in fifteen years, but for some unknown reason it sounded like a good idea at the time. John ordered three shots of Jezynowka, a blackberry brandy of Polish origin. It is very sweet and tastes a lot like cough medicine. I recalled the last time I'd had it was in high school in another moment of clouded, poor decision making. But I was among friends and figured, what the heck? It's only one shot.

The bartender lined them up and John made a toast.

"Well, here's to Muskie fishing, fellas!"

We all toasted and tossed back our shots.

Steve grimaced. "Ugh, that is not good."

"Mmmm, medicine," I joked, giving credence to the fact that drinking sometimes completely blots out previous bad experiences with a given liquor.

"Tastes a lot like cough medicine," I said.

Steve and John both laughed.

Half an hour later, John said, "Time for another shot?"

Now I have to step outside myself for a moment and recommend that if you ever hear those words, you simply run out the door of wherever you are, immediately. One shot is never a good idea, two are a path down a long, dark alley and any more than that is a brutal form of self-flagellation. Don't do it!

But we did.

We had a couple more rounds and the rest of the evening became hazy. Of that I am not proud. In my vacation high, I'd reached the point where my entire world was beer, dice and shots. Feeling invincible at the time, I figured I'd deal with the consequences in the morning. After all, it was only a little fishing. How hard could it be? No big deal. I got this.

The next morning came to my bedside and stood there wearing a dark gray cloak, reeking of death and remorse. My head sloshed and thrummed as John turned on the kitchen light. I lay there counting the drinks from the night before, as I tend to do when I am in the throes of a hangover. It was my attempt to reconcile my wretched condition against its cause. My counting only led to more self-loathing. None of this addressed the stark reality that sitting in a rocking boat all day seemed like the worst way to cure a hangover of this magnitude.

I went into the bathroom and popped a couple of ibuprofen and then went about my usual morning routine. We all went outside and hitched the boat to John's Isuzu Trooper and headed to the lake. I took the backseat hoping to catch some twenty second naps to ease my aching head when no one was looking. As we barreled down the highway, the trees whizzed by like telephone poles in a blur of green. County highways up north are two lanes of curvy rises and falls, pure punishment for anyone on the edge of sickness. John's radio pounded out Pearl Jam's "Even Flow," a song which, in any other circumstance, I loved. Now it seemed to be a sort of auditory punishment for my sins of the night before.

We stopped at Dietz' gas station to try and get some suckers to fish with over the course of our day. It was a lean year for sucker harvesting though, so Dietz' was fresh out. John made a quick call to Townline Sports, a short drive away, to see if they had any. They confirmed they did, so we got back in the truck and sped off to get some before they were all sold.

On the ride to Townline Sports, my stomach began to churn and roil.

Oh, no. You cannot puke in John's truck. Think happy thoughts.

Ten minutes later we pulled into the lot and got out. The fresh air felt good compared to the stale air of the Trooper. *Maybe I'll be okay after all.* We filed into the store with the bait bucket in hand. Inside was stiflingly warm compared to the brisk October air outside. The fact I was dehydrated from a night on the town may have played a role in my temperature sensitivity, but it feels better to blame it on an overheated store.

While we waited for the attendant to get the suckers, John looked at the selection of rods and talked with one of the sales staff. It was then the telltale mouth-watering started for me. You know the feeling. It's one every kid has experienced, usually in bed, right before a dash to the toilet to retch. We all know how it ends and it is best if you don't try and stifle it.

"I'll be waiting outside," I said.

Steve wandered out with me. Cognizant of being on the receiving end of an imminent weight loss, I sauntered over to the dumpster, trying to be sly and not give Steve any idea as to how bad I really felt. Maybe I could yak in the trash when he wasn't looking. I peeked in the dumpster, but the time wasn't right, and I thought I might be able to hold it down. Besides, I didn't want to linger and tip my hand altogether, so I turned away hoping I could tough this one out.

Steve was standing a few feet away when it finally happened. The watering mouth gave way to sudden uncontrollable cramps in my stomach signaling the gastro-geyser was about to blow. In a single motion that has since been termed "peacocking" by Steve and John, my head jerked back then forward like a whip being snapped. I hurled the entire contents of my roiling gut right there in the parking lot. Steve claims it had an arc to it big enough to cause its own rainbow. His post-event compassion is only outdone by his colorful recall of the circumstances. I'd never puked standing up before, so I can't speak to the spectator's perception of distance, projection or technique scoring. I only knew I felt instantly better as I stood spitting the residual stomach acid to the ground.

Steve stood there wide-eyed in disbelief, his mouth agape.

"Dude, did you just do what I just saw?"

"Yeah, that might have been me," I said with an acidic smile.

"What the hell? Why didn't you puke in the dumpster? You were right by it."

"I pondered the idea, but thought I might be able to hold it in."

"I can't believe you just booted," he said, still in apparent shock.

Just then, John strolled out of the store carrying a bucket full of suckers. As he approached, Steve said in a subdued voice, "Hey John, Jim just puked right in the parking lot."

John looked at me, then the ground, then back at me again.

"What the fuck? You feelin' better, now?" he asked.

"Yeah, actually. Like a new man," I admitted.

"I asked him why he didn't puke in the dumpster," Steve said. He seemed to be fixated on my lack of planning without much regard for how I felt now that it was over.

"Well, let's get out of here before someone sees it," John said, taking the suckers over to the boat and dumping them in the live well. Steve and I jumped in the Trooper and John negotiated his way back to the highway.

The rest of the ride to the lake was much more bearable. My stomach felt better, but my head still thumped. The ibuprofen had done little to help. It would be a long day on the boat, but I knew there were worse places I could be.

We got to the landing and the two of them set to work on getting the trailer backed and the boat launched. I was still new to this gig and clearly the third wheel. I did what

I could and tried to stay out of the way when I needed to. My main job was to hold the launch rope attached to the bow of the boat so when it was in the water, free of the trailer, I could pull it back to shore. In the fog of my hangover, I was obsessed with trying to untangle the long rope not realizing I was in the path of John's backing up of the trailer. Unannounced, John stopped, put the truck in park, got out, and came over to me.

"Are you okay?" he asked with a tone of intense irritation.

This was not a moment of sincere compassion from John. He was clearly annoyed and a little pissed off at my general in-the-wayness. It was one thing to be hungover and sick, but another to be a hindrance in moving toward our goal of fishing. John takes fishing very seriously and has little patience for ineptitude. My zombie-state was trending high in ineptness at the moment, and he wanted to make it clear.

"Uh, oh, sorry," I said awkwardly, stepping back out of the way of the trailer.

This was only my second-year fishing with John, and I was fairly shaken by his annoyance with me. I loved fishing for Muskies and was concerned I was wearing out my welcome and might not be invited in subsequent years. We'd had a blast together the night before and I thought the whole puking thing, and now this, had inked me indelibly on John's fecal roster, if you know what I'm saying.

His correction snapped me out of my fog, and we finished up with our launch. Once we were on the water, the two of them rigged up the suckers and I began casting out the front of the boat. I felt a little better being in the fresh air, working the lure through the water. The rhythmic repetition of cast, retrieve and repeat helped me focus on something other than my thumping head.

My continuous casting for the next hour and a half became hypnotic. My mind drifted and recalled how Steve mentioned he'd never caught one while casting, only on suckers while trolling. This caused me to think my efforts were in futility, so I became complacent with my casting and began to lose my focus. On one of my hundreds of retrieves, I felt a strike on my line just as the lure hit the water near the shore. I reared back with my rod and set the hook.

"Fish on!"

"What? Really?"

"Yes, get the net!"

Steve and John scrambled to get the big net unfolded and extended.

"Oh, it's just a little guy," I said.

I led the fish into the net anyway. We high-fived one another despite the small size. It was around twenty-four inches.

"Well, that was sorta disappointing. But it was a fish, anyway," I said.

"Jim, I have a saying. 'a Muskie is a Muskie,'" John said. To this day, I've always remembered that. They're still rare and difficult to catch, so no fish should be diminished. I was just happy to catch one for the second consecutive year and thought it might help to get me back into John's good graces again. We snapped a couple of photos and set the little guy free.

The catch actually helped me feel better, at least momentarily. It certainly took the edge off any tension in the boat that might have been lingering from our launch. Up to this point in the day, Steve and John had carried the conversation. I had been fairly quiet, as talking only seemed to amplify my headache. After I caught the fish though, I began to boast and trash talk a little more, like I'd done the night before at the bar.

"He must be feeling better. He's getting his spunk back," John noted.

"Yes, he is. I don't know if that is a good thing or not," Steve joked.

We all laughed, and it felt good. This sort of banter in the boat is much of what fishing is all about for me. Like the teasing and joking with Johnny Kaufenberg years before, the back-and-forth in the boat filled the time with moments that kept things light and fun. I was relieved to be back in John's good stead. Little did I know, he would become such a good friend. He and his wife Jen have opened their cabin for our visits over the past ten years, and as a group we've grown closer and closer. We have caught some tremendous fish over those years, and when we haven't, we've filled in the gaps with laughter and reminders that time with good friends is something to store up and treasure away. Steve, John and Jen have made my annual treks to Muskie country one of the highlights of my year.

* * *

In mid-October of 2011, six weeks after my brother Rob passed away having lost his battle with cancer, I went up to John's cabin with Steve for our annual "Muskie Fest." Since it was also the weekend of Rob's birthday, I thought it would be cool to catch one in his honor. I also knew the odds were largely against us, given the finicky nature of the species. Catching these fish is a numbers game and statistically I figured we were due for the inevitable year where we'd get skunked.

We drove up on Thursday evening and it rained the entire way. The next morning the forecast was for more wind and rain, but it didn't deter us from starting out on our favorite lake. It was the lake where I'd caught my first one, so I was banking on the promise of a couple years prior. We launched the boat and started out where we'd caught fish before. As we rowed, we had difficulty holding our line in the stiff northwesterly winds and light rain.

After a couple hours, Steve said, "This is nuts. We have to get off this lake and try somewhere else to get out of this wind." While I admitted the winds were bothersome, I was hesitant to change locales because of the productive history of this particular lake. Switching might jinx my whole plan. The weather had made Steve crabby, so he suggested we go into town to have lunch and regroup. I worried about the lost time on the water in pursuit of my goal, but nevertheless, we trailered the boat and headed into town to strategize.

We stopped at the Pea Patch in Manitowish Waters. Business was brisk with a Friday lunch crowd. We ordered a beer and some appetizers to take the edge off our morning. It certainly seemed to lighten Steve's mood. I agree no one likes fishing in the rain, but I was obsessed with giving it 100% in trying to catch a fish in tribute to Rob. When we finished lunch, John called and recommended we try Birch Lake and mentioned it had some protected bays. High-wind fishing dictates that you fish on the windward side of the lake where the water is calmer as it blows overhead. This new lake was untested by us, but after calling John, it seemed to be our best possibility. It was also close to our cabin, so we could bail out easily if conditions went downhill.

We drove fifteen minutes, launched and motored to a nearby shoreline where the winds were lighter and made our rowing much easier. I cast lures from the front of the boat while Steve kept a steady depth and an eye on the suckers trolling out the back. As in years past we typically alternated who took the first fish that bites on one of the suckers. This year, on a couple of occasions Steve reminded me it was his turn to take the first. Knowing how difficult these fish are to catch, let alone two of them, I figured this was the nail in the coffin of my expectations. For Steve to catch one would be an accomplishment; to catch a second for myself would be exponentially more difficult. Because Steve had orchestrated much of the trip, I tried not to show my disappointment and simply said with a laugh, "Okay, that's cool. Just means we'll have to catch two."

Temperatures were in the forties and a steady drizzle kept conditions adequately miserable. I'd discovered the benefits of really good rain gear a few years before, but even the hardiest of fishermen have their limits in the midst of no action and an all-day rain. Two hours into it, I began to wonder if our efforts of the day might end up as a bust. The afternoon was beginning to wane, and our situation grew dimmer. I cast my heart out, trying one after another of Rob's lures he'd given me after he found out his diagnosis was terminal. I was trying desperately to increase my odds at landing a fish.

Then, at 3:15 p.m., the trolling reel started clicking. Steve quickly stood up, tended the rod and grabbed the line to see if it was a weed.

"Yep, that's a fish, alright. Row us back toward it, Jim."

I climbed off the deck and into the middle seat and rowed us back toward the large bobber. I was ecstatic to have some action, even if it was to be Steve's fish. It meant, should we encounter another, it would be my turn. Steve steadied the rod and made sure it was a fish and not a false positive. When it came time to set the hook, Steve made one of the most selfless acts I've ever seen in all of my years of fishing. He handed me the rod and said, "Here you go. It's Rob's birthday. Catch him a fish."

I was dumbfounded.

"Are you sure?"

"Yep. This means a lot more to you than me, so bring it in."

Situations like this make me realize how lucky I am to have such a good friend. We get along great in the boat and have built many unforgettable memories over the years. As much as we joke and criticize each other at times, there is a mutual respect for each other's skills, especially when there is a fish on the line.

I took the rod from Steve and reeled up the slack. He grabbed the oversized Frabill net, extended it and got ready. When the fish started to move with the sucker, I put the rod tip near the top of the water, reared back, and set the hook using great force. I struggled to keep the fish from going under the boat, jeopardizing a line-break. After a short, zealous fight, I led it into the net. Steve and I hooted and high-fived each other. Our perseverance had paid off. It was a small thirty-six incher, but in my mind, it was still a great fish. More significantly, I caught it on Rob's birthday, a short six weeks after his passing. To make it even better, I caught it while wearing a sweatshirt his wife had given me after he died. The joy, sadness, exhilaration and relief all came crashing together to create a moment I will never forget, and I owed it all to my friend, Steve.

After a quick photo, we released the fish healthy to fight another day. We fist bumped and I thanked Steve again for his graciousness. I reiterated what it meant to me. I remembered what his wife Jill had said years before when I'd caught my first Muskie with Steve's help. She said, "Steve seriously enjoys helping other people catch fish. It's gratifying for him. He loves it." I certainly witnessed that declaration firsthand with this catch.

At this point in the day, we still had a few hours of sunlight and the fish had energized us, so we agreed to continue trying our luck. My hope, at this point, was that Steve would catch a fish and turn a good day into a great day. However, the realist in me knew the odds of it happening were strongly against us.

About an hour later we again heard the click-click-click of the trolling reel.

"Is that what I think it is?" I asked.

Steve checked the line, felt weight on it, and said, "Yes, sir. That's a fish."

The mad scramble started in the boat. I worked the oars and positioned us near where Steve's line was, then readied the landing net. He waited the allotted time then at the right moment conducted a textbook-like hookset. He fought the fish with intent and excitement, positioning it to where I could scoop it into the waiting net. We fist bumped again, exuberant we'd both landed fish within an hour of one another. Our success this day exceeded anything I could have imagined.

We took the fish from the net. It was a small, beautifully striped thirty-two-inch tiger Muskie. We snapped a photo, released it healthy and decided to call it a day. And what a day it had been! Steve, in one small way, helped me heal the pain of losing a brother. His own brother, Pete, had died ten months earlier of pancreatic cancer. Steve, in many ways, was still grieving his own loss and could certainly relate to my situation. While we shared in common the loss of brothers to cancer, this trip made me realize that fishing with a friend who felt like a brother, was the next best thing to fishing with one. There are many sacred, spiritual moments in the lifetime of a person, and this day spent in a boat in a steady rain with a good friend, immediately became one for me.

Dead Lake

*Trying to cast as far as the ol' man
the boy has to untangle
another bird's nest.*

In the '60s, my dad and five of his six brothers started a tradition that became known as the Landwehr Hunt. It was held in mid-October and took place in the remote regions outside of Fergus Falls, Minnesota near the tiny town of Dent. My dad and his brothers had a friend named Denny, who had a farmhouse and some land up there. The house was adjacent to Dead Lake that, according to Landwehr lore, was very tough to fish. I was told none of the uncles had ever caught anything out of it and declared it true to its name, dead.

I might qualify the tradition by mentioning, while the event was called the Landwehr Hunt, very little actual hunting ever went on. It's alleged that, for several years, no one even brought a gun. That's not to say there wasn't some occasional fishing and hunting, but the weekend was really intended as a get-together centered around drinking, card playing and catching up with one another. It was always a stag event with just the Landwehr brothers, and sometimes Denny.

At one of the events sometime after my dad was killed in 1967, the brothers started another tradition that went along with the hunt. One of them purchased a bottle of Cardenal Mendoza brandy. It was decreed that whenever one of the brothers passed away, the surviving siblings would pour a small shot to toast the fallen brother. Then, their name and date of death was inked on the outside of the wooden box that served as the packaging for the expensive brandy. Dad was first to be recognized in '67. Then the brandy sat for 26 years, before Uncle Dan passed away in 1993. One of the brothers was charged with keeping the bottle and bringing it up every year. It became a reverent tradition with a somber tone.

As the uncles slowly dropped off, the invitation to the hunt was extended to the eldest sons of the ones who had passed on. This was an attempt to keep family representation equal among the multi-generational attendees. My brother Tom served as our family representative for a number of years. The same held true for Steve, Uncle Dan's eldest, and Don, the son of Uncle Harry, the lone uncle who never attended the hunts because he claimed it "wasn't his thing."

Eventually the invitation broadened out to include any of the sons in my dad's generation. The uncles realized the importance of gathering as a family and determined time was of the essence. Though the farmhouse had a limited number of bedrooms, it had enough couches and floor space for all who could make the trek. Denny's farmhouse became Denny's flophouse for one weekend a year.

In 2006, my brothers decided all four of us should try and make the trip. In essence, it would constitute a comparable experience to dad and his brothers. The four of us would collectively sit around the table they sat around, sleep where they had slept, and metaphorically walk in their footsteps. Add to this the fact that three of the remaining uncles would be present, and it seemed like a good opportunity to reconnect with some extended family and see what the famed Landwehr Hunt was all about.

* * *

I committed to the trip and made arrangements with the brothers. After I drove the first five hours from southeastern Wisconsin to St. Paul, I hitched a ride with Rob from there to the hunt. When we walked into the farmhouse at about 5:00 p.m., the kitchen was warm and teeming with activity. Many of the men were enjoying a happy hour cocktail, some on their second or third. Jeans, flannel, and sweatshirts were the attire of the day, defense against the mid-October chill that bit aggressively this far north. My cousin Chris was busy at the stove prepping dinner for the group. Chris has gourmet-level skills but was working more on a feed-the-masses scale for this gathering.

"Well, look who's here! Robby and Jimmy!" Uncle Jim declared, using names we hadn't been called by in years.

"Hello everyone. It's good to be here," I said.

Rob had been up to the hunt the year before, so he was a familiar face to everyone present. I, on the other hand, was seeing relatives I literally had not seen in twenty years or more. I immediately recognized all the uncles, Jim, Willie and Tom, my dad's fraternal twin. My cousin, Bobby came over and gave us both man-hugs. He actually prefers the name Coe, and is one of the warmest, most genuine people I know. There is nothing more important to him than family, and it showed. He was always at every funeral and reached out to any and all family in their time of need. While his tendencies toward the wild rock-n-roll lifestyle have caused some family members to bristle at the mention of his name, most know his allegiances are true and his motives pure. He is the mortar between the bricks of all of us.

My cousin Don also came over to say hi and shake my hand. He is another one of the pillars in the family and was the key organizer of the whole event from year to year. Nothing made him happier than seeing his extended family together. This love for family became apparent through conversations with him and others over the course of the weekend. Don was well respected among the entire clan.

We all chatted for a bit and then a few of us stepped outside with our beers to get a little fresh air. Evening was on the doorstep and the air was crisp with those wispy, fish-bone clouds that so frequently float in the skies in autumn. Rob and I busted out the Backwoods cigars, a habit we only partook of when we were at a cabin or camping in the Boundary Waters. Our dad and grandfather were both cigar smokers, Dad occasionally and Grandpa more of a problem smoker. Sharing bad stogies at this location was a connection point between us, our father and his father. A nasty habit I know, but sometimes you gotta do what you gotta do. You have to die sometime, and if a once-a-year cigar with my brothers is my death ticket, well, I could think of worse ways.

Rob and I lit up while Coe opted for a cigarette. As we puffed away, Don spotted a deer stand out on the edge of the corn field and suggested we check it out. It was a self-standing structure, basically a small clubhouse atop a set of stilts. It was too good to resist for a bunch of guys with nothing better to do.

"To the deer stand," I said, raising my beer.

"To the deer stand," Rob echoed.

The group of us wandered over to the dwelling and climbed the steps. The inside was stark, but livable. It had four walls, a door and a few windows. Deer stands were built to be used a few weekends a year, and this one looked the part. I've never personally hunted deer, but these digs seemed a lot more appealing than sitting on a seat strapped to the trunk of a tree freezing my everything off.

Once we were in, Coe proposed a toast. "To family. Long live the Landwehrs."

"To family," we all echoed.

It was a toast in recognition of the beauty and the brevity of our time together. The fact that it was conducted in a deer stand was irrelevant. Our collective togetherness on that weekend was all that mattered. So, we puffed away, back slapped and, before long, the jokes and stories started rolling out. After a few minutes we started cracking open windows as a blue haze of smoke began collecting near the ceiling. It was quickly becoming like a bad house party from the seventies. One could almost believe an environment like this wasn't good for a person.

At the same time, it was like being nine years old again. Here we were, all the boys hanging out in a tree fort, minus the tree, doing all the illicit things we could handle. Beer, cigars and coarse talk, all punctuated by uncontrollable laughter. It was like the world's smallest frat party, and we didn't care. The only thing missing was blaring music and an appearance from the local police.

After about fifteen minutes of absolute depravity, we all needed to escape the hookah pipe in the sky we'd crawled into. We exited the stand single file back into the reality of adult life, reeking like a fire having been extinguished with dirty socks and mop water. I took a deep breath of northern Minnesota's finest air and made a mental note to remember this moment forever.

I fully recognize this was probably what most would call a juvenile moment among grown men, and that is fine. It is also one of those rocking chair memories that will cause me to grin deviously when I am sitting around the television at the nursing home watching Seinfeld reruns. It was a unifying moment between me, my brothers and my cousins whom I hadn't seen in a long time. We were taking full advantage of our time together. It was tomfoolery with a capital T, for sure. But these guys were my kin, cast in the mold of my father, who I never really knew. In some ways this moment was a connection back to him, a blood connection, and one I needed badly at the time. Those moments in the deer stand were the start of an almost supernatural weekend.

* * *

After our connective moment in the stand, we walked back to the farmhouse. Inside Chris announced it was time for dinner. Everyone took a seat and Uncle Tom led us in a prayer. He was a lifelong devoted Catholic and likely the most spiritual person at the table, so it seemed a good fit. We all said our amens and, before we dug in, proposed a toast to all those who'd gone before us. It was a moving recognition of the sanctity of the occasion, as well as the location itself. We had much to be thankful for, not the least of which was the breath we all breathed.

After a delicious meal and a multitude of simultaneous conversations, talk began to circulate about making a run into Dent. The town was just a short drive away. There were a couple of bars, and it was Friday night, so it sounded like a good idea. Coe's friend James was along for the weekend, and he was a teetotaler with a pickup truck, so we had ourselves a designated driver. The rest of the guys piled into a couple of other vehicles, and we caravanned to the bustling metropolis of Dent, population 192.

We filed into the bar and found our seats. I was shocked when I saw uncles Tom and Willie walk in. They were both in their seventies and doing their best Keith Richards imitations in the name of tradition and pilgrimage. For me, it was just cool to be there. My father's death at a young age had distanced our St. Cloud relatives from us by the sheer nature of geography. We lived in St. Paul, an hour and a half from them, so we only made the trip up there a couple of times a year, at most. Being back together with many of them in these remote regions of Minnesota felt heartwarming and good.

What transpired that night was a whole lot of shenanigans and shall remain largely untold. Billiards were played, stories of past trips were regurgitated, and pull tabs were pulled, some lucky, most not. After the bar closed, we headed back to the farmhouse. Paul thought it was time to show me the infamous round barn that sat on the property.

"Jim, have you been in the round barn yet?" Paul asked.

"No, I haven't, but I'd like to."

Paul turned to Rob and said, "Hey, we're going to the round barn, want to come?"

"Sure. I think we need a beer though," Rob replied.

"Well, that goes without saying," Paul added.

We all grabbed a beer and walked out to the barn. It was a fantastic structure that had recently been renovated to more of a showpiece than an actual functioning building. The roof work and architecture were an amazing testament to the generation before us who built it. It was cathedral-like and spectacular. Paul remarked it would be a great venue for a concert with all of the inherent acoustics the round roof provided. None of us was sure of the purpose in designing a round barn, but there must have been a reason for it. Also, it might be noted the round portion was actually joined to a large rectangular section giving it the shape of a lollipop from the sky. In any case, the whole structure was dazzling.

As we toured the dim recesses of the barn it was hard not to picture the folks who'd worked with the animals and feed over the years. None were relatives of course, but it gave me a sense of appreciation for the hard life of a farmer as I walked through the cool, musty confines. Eventually, we came to a sloped, concrete slab.

"It's my understanding this is the killing floor where they slaughter the piggies," Paul said with a straight face.

Rob and I looked at him in shock and horror.

"What? Really?"

"Yep. You know those baby back ribs that taste so good? Well, this is where those baby pigs end up. Their blood runs down this slab into this little gutter here."

Then, Paul made a squealing pig sound, "Ree, ree, ree!"

Rob and I busted up. I couldn't stop laughing. It was not out of disrespect for the pigs, but rather a reaction to Paul's delivery of the piglet response. Seeing us laugh, he did it again.

"Ree, ree, ree!"

We continued with our wild laughter. Dark humor like this is my weakness. It fell into the realm of Kurt Vonnegut's "So it goes," references to every death that happened in his book *Slaughterhouse Five*.

So it goes...

Ree, ree, ree!

The rest of those early morning hours were laced with moments like this. Riotous laughter and banter between myself and my brothers. It was adult nonsense with tinges of juvenility, and it was all positively therapeutic. I'd go as far as to say I've never laughed that hard in my life. It felt like a great release, an orgasm of laughter. There in that roundhouse, I was 500 miles from home, but amongst the love and camaraderie of my brothers, it felt like what home used to be. It was the reason I'd come up to the hunt, and I was grateful I'd made the trip.

* * *

The next morning, I woke up facing the debt collection of the previous night's alcoholic binge. The aroma of breakfast cooking downstairs wafted into my bedroom. I knew I should probably join the more responsible family members who had risen and gathered around the table, but my head was pounding as I lay there replaying the events of the night before. I figured I had a couple of brothers who were sharing my agony, so I tried to get back to sleep. After tossing and turning for another hour, I finally gave up and rose to face the day and live out the consequences of my over-imbibing. My hangovers always come with a healthy dose of self-loathing, and this one was no different. When would I ever learn?

When I got downstairs, most of the breakfast crowd had finished and moved on to other things. A couple of the guys were off hunting and others were sprinkled about the house or outside in conversation. Uncle Jim was still around the table with his coffee. As I ate a light breakfast, I talked with him about my dad. I mentioned that I did not know much about him or his past.

"Well, Roy was probably bipolar, you know," Jim said.

"Really?"

"Oh my gosh, yes! He was up and down his whole life. Beyond a doubt, Jimmy. Definitely prone to depressive episodes."

"Wow, I never knew that, but I guess you would know, having lived with him"' I said.

"Yeah, and ultimately it was what led to his downfall. He was a tortured soul, so to speak."

"That is interesting. I knew he had issues after our sister Linda died, but I didn't think there was anything prior. That's why conversations like these are so important. They allow me to get the perspective of those who knew him, other than my immediate family. Everyone has a different take on his life."

Jim went on to tell me a couple of stories about Dad. As hard as it was to hear his description of my dad's tumultuous life, it was equally fascinating. His stories were a window into a mysterious part of my family lineage. They were also representative of the takeaways a person gets when gathering with relatives around a table or a fire pit. I know if my dad was still alive, he'd have been here with us. Instead, I was sharing his life through his brothers and coming to understand him a little better as a result. It was exactly where I needed to be at that moment in my life. A poignant discussion on an October morning in the middle of nowhere.

* * *

After breakfast, the group dispersed to various activities sprinkled around the cabin and grounds. Coe and his friend James said they were going to shoot some target practice in the back forty of the farm. Rob and Paul said they would join him. This riled up Uncle Tom, mostly because there was a longstanding rule among the brothers, there would be no shooting outside of actual off-site hunting. An even more explicit rule was, there was to be no drinking and guns combined. Ever. A common-sense rule, but one that was put in place for good reason.

"You know the rules, Coe. No drinking and guns!"

"I know, Tom. We won't be drinkin'. We're just going out back to do a little target practice."

"Well, I don't like it. Be careful, whatever you do," Tom emphasized.

Coe asked if I wanted to go along, and I declined. I've always been a rule follower and didn't want my uncle to think less of me on my first trip to the hunt.

"I think I'm going to do a little fishing instead," I said.

"Good luck with that, Jimmy. In all the years we've been coming up here, no one's ever caught anything. There's a reason they named it Dead Lake," Uncle Jim said.

"Well, I'll never know unless I try," I said as I zipped my coat and headed out the door.

I ambled down to the shore and baited my hook with a large minnow and heaved it into the lake. The wind was cold and steady from the northwest. Like any native Minnesotan, I had packed my winter coat despite the fact it was only October. Fall weather can change quickly and snowflakes are never completely out of the question after September.

I stood there, hands in my coat pockets and watched the bobber do its thing. Shots periodically rang out from the area where the guys had gone shooting. After a half hour of futility, I went into the farmhouse to warm up. My cousin Chris was hanging out in the kitchen.

"Any luck?" he asked.

"No, not yet. I came in to get out of the wind for a bit."

"Yeah, that wind is relentless."

"Sure is. The gales of November in October," I joked.

We chatted for a few minutes, again connecting with a cousin I didn't see very often. When I told him I needed to check my line, he said he'd come along with me. He put on his coat, and we walked over to the lake, where I'd left my rod. As I approached the steep bank leading down to the lake, I saw my bobber zigzagging across the water.

"Hey, I think I might actually have a fish on," I said as I scrambled down the embankment.

"It sure looks that way," Chris said.

I grabbed the rod and set the hook. After a short, spirited fight, I pulled in a small 24" northern pike.

"Well, would you look at that! I don't remember anyone catching anything up here in the years I've come," Chris said.

"It's not much of a fish, but I guess given the history of this lake, I'll take it. Hey, could you get a picture of it, so I have proof for my brothers?"

"Sure can."

I handed Chris my digital camera and he snapped a shot of me holding the "lake snake" as we call those small, pesky pike. As I set it free, Chris said he was going back up to the warmth of the farmhouse. I told him, now that I had a fish, I was going to check out the target practice. We parted ways and I set my fishing rod down and walked in the direction of the shots.

When I approached the makeshift firing range Rob was taking aim with a shotgun in the direction of a set of ten bowling pins set on the ground about thirty feet away. The firing range was laid out against the backdrop of a thick forest, in the name of safety. Furthermore, the guys were shooting downward, so any slugs would ultimately end up in the dirt near the pins. When Rob was done shooting, I showed everyone the picture of my fish. They were all equally impressed by the fact I'd caught anything in the lake, and unimpressed by the size of the fish itself. I had to take the victory for what it was.

It seemed I'd stumbled into the middle of a sport the group had invented the year before called shotgun bowling. Coe and James had salvaged a complete set of pins from a bowling alley demolition and brought them along just for the occasion. The concept behind shotgun bowling is exactly as it sounds. You get two shots to knock down the pins. It is also exactly as redneck-hillbilly as it sounds, though I will admit we did keep track of strikes and spares. So, there was that.

Now, let me be clear. I consider myself to be a cultured guy. I love museums, art and going to the theater. I write poetry, marvel at the eloquent significance of an orangey sunset over the rolling waves of the Pacific Ocean, and even appreciate the instrumental overlays in a piece of music by Beethoven. I am all about those things. They are what make life rich and worthwhile.

At the same time, there might be an equally soft spot in the recesses of my perpetually juvenile cerebral cortex for the sport of cretins called shotgun bowling. It provides a chance for men to return to their youth, where making noise with powder and shot in the name of knocking something down is a form of amusement. Given the fact we were taking safety precautions and not harming the local wildlife, it made it seem like an almost legitimate form of recreation. Or, if not, at least one step above complete redneck. If pressed, one could argue it was an easier form of trap shooting.

Coe handed me a pair of earplugs which I promptly put in as I watched my brother Paul shoot a frame and try to pick up the spare with his second shot. When you boiled it down, it was actually just a slow-moving, duller form of regular bowling. As the birdshot hit the pins, they simply fell back clonking each other with little effect. There was none of the ricochet or accompanying cacophonic echoes one gets in the confines of a bowling alley. It was a climactic anticlimax.

After they'd finished, Coe brought out his .44 magnum. This is the long-barreled handgun made popular by Clint Eastwood in his Dirty Harry movies of the '70s. Prior to loading it, Coe let us all hold it and feel the heft of the cold steel in our hands. I'd never held a gun of that size before, so was both intrigued and a little frightened by its imposing weight and craftsmanship.

Ever since I was young, I've always had a healthy fear of guns. Coupled with my pacifist nature and the fact I'm a lousy shot, I've never aspired to become a hunter or marksman. I have owned a couple of shotguns in the past, but they were clearly tools put in my path to serve as reminders of how inept I was on the offensive side of a gun. I'm convinced certain people just should not be allowed to own or handle a gun, and I am definitely one of them.

That said, I had to shoot this .44 magnum. Just once.

"That is an awesome looking gun, Coe."

"Thanks. Want to try it out?"

"Um, yes, please. I just want to shoot it once. Mostly to be able to say I did."

"Okay. Suit yourself. Let me load it for you," he replied.

The other reason behind only wanting to shoot it once was because I couldn't get Uncle Tom's voice out of my head about the danger of guns and breaking the Landwehr Hunt rules. Even though no one was drinking, I still felt like I was violating a long-standing commandment of the Landwehr brothers' hunt-guild, where guns were only to be used for actual hunting. I am the world's biggest rule follower. My guilt was crippling.

I put on the earmuffs as Coe loaded the revolver and handed it to me carefully. He warned that I should hold the gun with both hands as it packed quite a kick. I took a wide stance, extended my arms in the direction of the head pin and sighted down the long barrel. I slowly squeezed the trigger. Kaboom! The kick of the gun was even more significant than I expected. All the pins stood there unscathed taunting me, an unpleasant reminder of why guns will never be anything more than a dangerous intrigue to me.

The guys all laughed as I lowered the gun to a safe position pointing at the ground.

"Wow! That is something else. I don't know about the rest of you, but the only thought I have coming away from this is I would not want to be on the receiving end of a bullet from this thing. Man!" I said, handing the gun back to Coe. "Thanks for letting me try it."

Rob, Paul and James stood there with grins on their faces. Previously, they had all taken their turns shooting the magnum. Their grins showed they were squarely in the camp of humble respect for the power and danger inherent in wielding such a deadly weapon. They all laughed and nodded. We seemed to share in the knowledge that, while it was harmless to shoot at a bunch of bowling pins, none of us would likely be willing to point it at another human being and pull the trigger. Or maybe it was just me.

After my shot, I stuck around for another couple of shooters, then walked back to the farmhouse. My inherent fear and respect for guns had been reaffirmed and I was again reminded why I am a fisherman and not a hunter, as evidenced by my crappy aim. Besides, I'd come this far in life without shooting myself or someone else, so I figured it was probably best to quit while I was ahead.

* * *

My cousin Don continued to orchestrate the Landwehr Hunt for years after my one and only experience with it in 2006. It changed venues as necessary, but always focused on getting the uncles, cousins and brothers together no matter where the location. He always included me on the invitation because he knew how important it was to get as many of us together as possible. However, the event usually took place in mid-October, which was always in direct conflict with my Muskie fishing. While I appreciated the significance of the hunt and spending time with extended family, after I caught my first, nothing could get between me and that annual venture.

At the same time, I am incredibly grateful I did take that one trip to Fergus Falls. It gave me the chance to sit in the same room as my father had over forty years earlier. In talking to my uncles, I felt I'd come to know my dad a little better, both his good qualities and his struggles. But perhaps the biggest takeaway of all was the recognition of love between the brotherhood of men gathering for no other reason than to share in the comradery of what it meant to be a Landwehr. It is hard to put a value on something like that.

Grand Lake

Creaking with the waves
the old dock holds memories
now long forgotten.

Without a doubt, the most unique cabin I've ever spent time in is situated on Grand Lake, outside of St. Cloud, Minnesota. The cottage holds a special place in my heart, largely because it was built by my paternal grandfather, Adolph, in 1934. When he was too old to maintain it, he sold it to my aunt Mariette, the eldest of his children. Mariette eventually passed it on to her own daughter, Laura, making it a three-generation cottage.

The structure is unlike traditional cabins namely because the logs are positioned vertically, not horizontally. Stained a dark brown and held together by a bright white mortar the timbers gave the cabin a sense of lift. I'd like to say this was grandpa's creative side shining through his otherwise stoic German heritage. After all, trees grow vertically, so why not build a cabin that reflects it? Makes sense to me.

Aunt Mariette was always gracious about inviting family up to her cottage. After my father passed, she made it a point to try and get one or two of us Landwehr kids up there for a few days in the summer. It gave Mom a break from some of her burdens, so it was worth the hour and a half drive each way to drop us off and pick us up.

Though I was quite young at the time, I have vivid memories of making the trek to a fishing hole with my cousin. As we walked down the dirt road, horseflies feasted on our necks and heads. When they weren't landing on us, they were furiously buzzing around us. It was my first exposure to these evil insects, and it was mighty unpleasant. My cousin and I took to running ahead ten yards then ducking and running backwards in an attempt to fool the pesky beasts. It was only a matter of time before they found us and resumed their annoyance.

One summer, after my sister spent the weekend up there, she told me Mariette and her husband, Virgil, had thrown a pot party at the cottage.

"A pot party? Really? Who all was there?" I asked.

Aunt Mariette, Uncle Virgil and a few of their friends," Jane replied.

My jaw dropped at the thought that my aunt and uncle were not only pot smokers, but they threw pot parties for their friends. The thought of their cabin being filled with the smoke of the Devil's Lettuce shocked me. Oh, the horrors! I'd always thought them to be too old and conservative to be lawbreaking drug users.

I pressed Jane for details. "Was it rowdy? Did people spend the night? What did the neighbors think?"

It was only after significant questioning I found out the "pot party" was actually in reference to the installation of an indoor toilet to replace the outhouse in the backyard. I couldn't believe the level of disconnect between Jane and myself to get that far off track. I was always a gullible kid, and my siblings would argue I could be a bit of a fog sometimes. It was misunderstandings like the pot party that made me realize maybe there was something to this fog.

* * *

The cottage at Grand Lake will probably be most remembered as the site of the Landwehr family reunions that took place every five years. Aunt Mariette always felt that getting family together was incredibly important. Though the cottage was not huge, there was lots of yard space and a beach area for people to congregate and talk. Of course, the history of the structure and the fact it was built by Grandpa Adolph made it the perfect location, meaningful across the generations.

One of the more recent reunions was held in 2015. Donna and the kids had commitments back in Wisconsin, so I drove to the Twin Cities alone and spent the night at my brother's condo. We planned to drive up to Grand Lake the following day. I figured the trip would give us a chance to catch up with each other during the drive. It would be our little two-person reunion before the actual event.

Because my immediate family were all out-of-towners, Laura arranged for us to stay overnight at a neighboring property as a sort of mini vacation. She was friends with the neighbor who was kind enough to lend the use of his house. Paul and I were relegated to the basement which had a couple of bedrooms. It was a nice accommodation by the neighbor that would allow us all to socialize into the late hours of the reunion if it were to happen.

When we arrived, two of my female cousins were stationed at a long table that served as a check-in area. It was where you were welcomed, paid for your lunch, given a nametag and details about the event. Beyond it, the backyard lawn teemed with activity. Relatives milled around chatting, some with drinks in hand, some not.

These family reunions were always large affairs, but this one in 2015 was the largest I'd seen. Dad had seven siblings and most of them had gone on to have large families as well. Judging from the number of small children, it was clear the third generation, that of my own kids, had moved into the child-bearing years.

I am terrible with names, so I was glad to see everyone had name tags. More importantly, the tags included the Landwehr parent-of-descent so people could make the connection to the family lineage. Mom always said there were so many cousins on the Landwehr side there were probably some we hadn't even met yet. It was true back in the day and likely more so now that they'd moved far and wide all over the country. I knew many of the cousins by sight, but when it came to their kids and grandkids, all bets were off.

After our initial introduction, Paul and I went in different directions, picking up conversations with our immediate family as well as relatives we hadn't seen since the last reunion. I wandered into the cottage at one point and took a look around. It was much like I remembered it as a boy. Game bird and fish taxidermy mounts hung from the walls around the living room. Uncle Tom was an avid taxidermist, and his work lent a nice up-north feel to the place. Above the kitchen door hung the biggest largemouth bass I'd ever seen. On top of his adept taxidermy skills, Tom was a capable hunter and fisherman as these mounts were proof.

The unique architecture of the cottage held a certain mystique for me. The tall, vertical timbers held tight by brilliant white mortar gave the place felt sacred like a cathedral. It was almost as though it was built as a testament to the gifts of a forest and the natural world. If the cabin was a cathedral, then the families on site were its congregation, all gathered for this five-year high Mass.

The reunion crowd took on a life of its own. People came and went in and out of small groups gathered in both the back and front yards. Our get-togethers were always a little strange for me, talking to people I only see every five years, some of them barely recognizable. I tend to enter these situations with great trepidation, but always come away glad I'd made the effort. These folks are my tribe and my kin. Knowing a little more about them or reestablishing our connections was important and reminded me we were all doing our best to carry the torch of our forebears.

One of the more interesting artifacts on display was Grandpa Adolph's leather-upholstered rocker. My cousin acquired the chair and kept it in his basement after Grandpa died. He'd made a point to bring it up to the reunion, knowing many people would recognize it. The chair was scarred with a number of cigar burns in between the tacks holding the leather tight to the arms. Grandpa was a big cigar smoker and known for his love of strong drink as well. I have boyhood memories of him sitting in the chair when we went to visit him in St. Cloud. I remember the rocker when the burns were still being made, so it was nostalgic to see it was still around.

A few of the family, including myself, took photos seated in the classic rocker. It was a small fragment of Landwehr family history. I've often wondered what the story behind each of the burns might be. What was grandpa going through at the time? What were his struggles? Family? Job? Sickness? The burns hold stories of our past, stories once lived but never spoken. Those tales were taken to the grave of the man who built this cottage, and perhaps that's where they belonged.

At one point during the afternoon, I was chatting with one of my cousins, and, for the life of me I cannot remember who. As I said, these are people I only see once every five years. I do know it was someone I'd never really talked to one-on-one before.

Having released my first memoir, *Dirty Shirt*, the year before, the conversation drifted to it. The book recounts my experiences in the Boundary Waters Canoe Area Wilderness and how it provided a connection point for my brothers and me to our deceased father. Because of his early death, none of us boys ever really knew him, so the shared experience of an area he loved was as close as we could get to doing that. Somewhere along the way, the conversation turned to my dad and the night he was killed.

This cousin provided details I'd never heard before, even down to some of the words passed before my father was assaulted and eventually killed. I didn't know how to process what I was hearing, and, frankly, didn't think to ask him what his sources were. These were newly disclosed, yet unverified details to a traumatic event, one I'd been forced to come to grips with and reconstruct in my mind a thousand times before. His account threw a curveball at my whole paradigm, and I didn't know what to make of it. Instead, I simply filed it away as another possible scenario from that tragic night in June of 1967.

Over the course of my life, the story of his beating and death has taken on all the clarity of a UFO sighting for me. There were some that witnessed it, others that heard about it and have changed details with every telling. And there were still others that want to believe they saw it badly enough that they'd convinced themselves they had. In actuality there were two eyewitnesses that I know of. One a bartender, the other a waitress who recounted the story to my sister Jane in a phone call decades later. Her account, along with the bartender's version told to my mother, both aligned with my father being in the wrong place at the wrong time. He was an innocent in a random, racially motivated attack. To formulate my own closure, I am inclined to believe the accounts of those who were there over a third party relative a generation removed.

The conversation with my cousin was one among many the day brought forth. It is these discussions of family tragedy mixed in with those of joy, struggle and personal triumph that make reunions so important. They are a reuniting of people from the same bloodline in the name of recounting our past and injecting positive energy and love into the future of one another.

In these present days where history has been deemed less relevant with the rise of technology, family history passed on through the oral tradition is a breath of fresh air. And while the details are sometimes lost or the facts jumbled, the beauty is found in the sharing. For it is in the human connections reignited in person-to-person exchanges which forms the foundation of what makes a family different than any other group. It is why we were gathered in a small, quirky cottage in Rockville, Minnesota on a hot summer day.

* * *

Evening came on with a gentleness and a stunning sunset over Grand Lake. There was little to no breeze and temps in the low 70s. It was one of the two dozen nice evenings Minnesota gets in a summer. I say this in jest to emphasize how nice it really was. If you've ever lived there, you know. You never leave the house without a sweatshirt, and you keep the ice scraper in your car year-round.

Mom, Pat, Jane, Paul, and I all grabbed cocktails and pulled up lounge chairs along the lakeshore. As we sat, we talked about some of the relatives we'd seen and mingled with at the reunion. We mentioned how good it was to see some of the old timers, like Aunt Fran and Uncle Tom, my father's fraternal twin. We talked about memories of this place, the nerve center or nucleus of the small, but vibrant Landwehr universe. And, naturally, we re-told family stories told countless times before. It felt good to revisit them just the same.

The sunset yielded to a beautiful moonrise. The temps cooled slightly as we all upgraded to long sleeves. The whole scene, with the lake, the moon and much of my family gathered conversing was idyllic and comforting. We talked for hours on every subject under the moon. Inevitably a few untold stories of our youth came out, stories we'd held from Mom for forty years or more. Tales including my near-miss run-ins with the law during my days in high school, as well as a few from Pat and Jane.

Of course, Paul's were the most shocking. Of all of us wild children, he was perhaps the wildest. One of his stories involved an attempt at putting a motorcycle in a car trunk in the wee hours of the morning near Grand Avenue. The story is best told by him, so forgive me for leaving out specifics of how, and perhaps more importantly, why? Frankly, the whole experience sounds like something straight out of a Hunter S. Thompson novel.

Mom's jaw dropped repeatedly as we all bore the sins of our youth. They were confessions before our mother Saint Mary, and we were all grateful she hadn't known about them at the time they happened. She always refers to those years in our house on Portland Avenue as the "black hole years."

Entire months and years a blur, caused in part by the fog six kids will create for any parent. She was too busy trying to keep food on the table and build a career to keep tabs on all six of us as we careened through our teens and twenties. We all turned out fine in the end, but it would be fitting to say God had a hand in all of it.

While it's true our mother was a living saint, it is also true she was protected by a legion of angels. This time on the beach, with the airing of our sins amidst the echoes of laughter across a glassy lake, was a reminder there are moments of heaven right here on earth among the sinners and saints. This sacrament of confession spoken and received was testament to the fullness of the lives we'd made in the shadow of those whose footprints were imprinted in the sand all around.

Unnamed Creek

*It's best to go
to the water to learn
how to catch the fish.*

In 2018, my wife asked if I would be interested in a two-night getaway at a cabin in central Wisconsin, near Hancock.

"We could just chill. You could use the time to write, and I'll just hang out and read. It'd be nice to get out of town," she said.

"You don't have to ask me twice. Make it happen!" I replied.

She swung into action and booked a two-night stay in October through vrbo.com, a website designed to provide vacationers with rental options all over the country.

Hancock is located in central Wisconsin, an area of the state I've passed through many times but one I am not familiar with. It is flat and non-descript from a car window. From what I'd seen it was primarily crop fields stretching for miles in every direction with tall stands of conifers forming windbreaks along the edge of fields. These stands were planted to help prevent the fertile, rich soils from blowing away. Occasional signs warned of the danger of low visibility during dust storms driven by high winds. In farm country, dirt is money, so keeping it in place is critical.

As we traversed the highway that ran parallel to Interstate 39, I began to question how this "cabin" could ever be in the woods. There seemed to be nothing but flat fields for miles in every direction. I am a purist. Call me old fashioned, but when I go to a cabin, I want it to be among the trees. Trees provide a sense of seclusion and buffer for a person. As importantly, it is healthy for my soul knowing I am amongst these towering, living things. For me pines and birch are almost sentient beings. They are sacred and give me peace.

We pressed on and continued to follow the reassuring voice on the Google Maps app. It routed us along the winding back highways of central Wisconsin. Eventually my fears were allayed when we were enveloped in a stand of pine trees that closed around us. It was a stark transition from the flat, irrigated fields we'd come from into the protective cover of the woods. I breathed a sigh of relief.

When we pulled into the driveway, we saw a quaint little cabin tucked among the pines. It was late afternoon and the light cast long, slanting shadows of the trees. The air scintillated clean and pure. It was instantly different from city air. Even though we were not way up north, we were up north! The other immediate difference was the evident quiet. We are bombarded with auditory pollution in our urban lives, so when that is absent, we suddenly have time to hear our inner voices. Those voices no longer need to shout over traffic noise, sirens, earbuds, telephones or the latest Netflix binge.

"Listen to the quiet. Isn't this nice?" I said, as we made our way toward the front door.

"Yes. So peaceful," Donna replied.

I looked around and noticed how remote we were from the main road and other cabins.

"I hate to say it but, as set back from the road and everything else, this would be the perfect spot for a murder."

"Well, that's a creepy thought to have," Donna replied.

"Sorry, it's just so quiet and remote. I don't know what made me think of it," I said.

I tried to put the thought out of my mind, but in one form or another, it stuck with me for the entire two-night stay. This is the kind of fear a country full of guns and mass shootings instills in a person.

We walked in to find a comfortable and charmingly cozy home. The kitchen was small but seemed to have everything necessary for the simple meals we'd packed. The main living area was furnished with a hodge-podge of comfortable chairs, lamps in their golden years and an assortment of end tables. In the center, on a brick foundation, hulked a large wood-burning stove serving as the focal point of the room. It was clearly set as a showpiece, a welcome substitution for the modern-day equivalent, a flat-screen TV. A throw rug lay on the front side of the fireplace at the foot of a brown leather couch, a perfect place to relax and watch the flames bite and flick.

The dining area was restricted to a small, compact table with fold-down leaves off the main living area. When opened it turned a two-person dinette into one suitable for four. The whole place was a collection of has-been furniture that probably once served a nobler role in a house elsewhere before being relegated to this cabin. Cabins are where all run-of-the-mill furniture goes to die.

The living room had a large sliding door that opened to a spacious deck overlooking the woods out back. I immediately made note of it as a nice place to do some writing if the weather held out. The outdoors helps the mind breathe and brings newfound inspiration. Unfortunately, Wisconsin weather changes quickly, making it difficult to sit comfortably for more than a couple of hours.

In some ways, the place was charming for what it lacked. So often, cabins are modernized to the point of detriment. To me, part of the whole experience is the presence of inconvenience. A shortage of electrical outlets, a mishmash of culinary tools or silverware, or dimly lit corners in need of a good standing lamp. Two-year-old magazines, a coffee maker with no auto-shutoff and a hanging wicker lamp right out of the 70s. These things might infuriate some people, but I find them as pleasant reminders of the past. As a sappy nostalgic, they take me back to a time when life was lived fully outside the range of a good Wi-Fi signal, or the reach of a cable box. I'm weird that way.

We unpacked the car and settled into our home away from home. I plopped into the aged Barcalounger and adopted it as my writing spot for the next two days. Meanwhile, Donna stretched out on the leather couch with her Kindle. The two of us have mixed feelings about the technology. We both love the feeling a paperback gives us as readers, but we've also discovered there is something to be said for the ease of packing a Kindle and never being without a book to read. Much like the cabin we were in, our lives have become a mix of the old and the new. Pulp and ink, pages and pixels. I'd go as far to say if there's a bad way to read, I've yet to find it. Reading makes *everyone* a better person.

After a simple dinner, we returned to our places in the living room. The tall pines cast their long shadows in the waning hours of sunlight.

"Should I start a fire?" I asked, dying to add to the ambience of our cozy home.

"Yeah, that might be nice," Donna replied.

I set to work assembling a fire in the cast-iron fireplace. After a few minutes the flames snapped and curled as I added larger kindling and eventually worked up to full-sized logs. When it was self-sustaining, I closed the doors and gazed at the flames. There is something primal about watching a fire. It speaks to the human spirit, equal parts warmth and visual fixation. We are forced to channel our inner caveman.

Donna and I read and wrote in relative silence into the night hours. This time together provided quiet and much-needed mental and intellectual therapy. Our mutual adoration—often times spent in total silence in the company of each other - is an integral part of what has kept us together for nearly thirty years. Our collective silence energizes us.

* * *

The next day was spent in much the same manner. At one point in the afternoon, I decided to take a break from my writing and try my hand at fishing. My research before the trip revealed there was a stream essentially in the backyard of the cabin. In anticipation of this, I'd packed my angling equipment. I grabbed my rod and a small case of spinners and went looking for a willing trout.

I had my doubts because I hadn't done much trout fishing in my past. My first real exposure to fishing exclusively for trout came years earlier in 2013 when my brother Tom invited me and my kids to fish near Lanesboro, Minnesota.

"Me and the kids go down with a couple other friends and have a blast every spring," Tom said.

"But neither I nor the kids have fly rods or waders," I replied.

"You don't need either of those. You can fish from shore and use regular equipment and a real small spinner. It's dynamite."

His offer sounded appealing, so I took him up on it. Despite very few fish, it gave me a taste of the sport, including the attendant difficulties and challenges which are part of it. I managed to land two of the smallest Brown Trout in the history of fishing, however. One would think this would dissuade me from ever wanting to pursue trout again. In reality, it had much the opposite effect. Like my first muskie, my first trout suddenly hooked me on a new sport.

The stream behind the Hancock cabin was at the bottom of a steep embankment. Overgrown with brush, the water taunted me from below, beckoning me to test it. Never one to ignore this calling to wet a line, I clambered down the bank, carefully avoiding roots threatening to send me headlong into a freefall. I wasn't out to catch my limit, but rather to prove I could catch a trout at all. Doing it without braining myself in a wicked fall would be a win-win.

When I reached the stream, it was apparent this would be no easy effort. Trees and brush presented obstacles from every direction. Eventually, I found a small clearing and cast into the stream. I immediately snagged a large, submerged log which I'd mentally made a note to avoid just a few seconds prior. After a short struggle and a few salty words, I freed the lure, promising myself to avoid it on future casts. I was unaware of the log's super-magnetic field that would unleash its pull on my lure every fourth cast or so. These repeated snags tested my patience and drained my deep well of expletives. It seems I took abnormal delight in testing my ability to not catch the log by catching the log.

After thirty minutes, I felt a tug on my ultralight. In a state of complete disbelief, I reeled in a small trout, not much bigger than my hand. I say disbelief because like my previous trout fishing attempt in Minnesota, I'd gone into it with the expectation I wouldn't catch anything. Fishing in swiftly moving water is difficult and I was new to it, so I figured I was just killing time in order to say I tried. To actually catch something was fairly astounding.

I was suddenly a living example that any fishing hack can catch a trout. It seemed like all a person needed to do was get out and try. Yes, it helps to have decent equipment, but when it comes right down to it, you can't catch a trout if you don't fish for one. Just get out there and figure it out. Contrary to my initial belief, there's nothing magical about it.

Now, the only thing worse than not catching a fish, is catching one right before you're ready to quit. This spurs a fisherman on to reckless things like continuing to snag the log they'd snagged for the previous fifteen minutes in the insane hope they might catch another trout. Sometimes they catch one, but more often it results in another half hour of their life lost to the futility of their experience before the one-and-only fish gave them hope.

In the end, every trip to a new location lays the opportunities before a person to learn something not only about the place, but also about themselves or their traveling companion. The Hancock cabin opened my eyes to the reminder I shouldn't judge a place based on my preconceived notions about it. Prior to this trip, I'd written off this part of the state as a flat agricultural plain. During our stay, it proved to me that beauty, solitude and contentment can be found almost anywhere if a person is open to it. In this case it was a quaint cabin among tall pines in the middle of farm country with the unexpected bonus of a trout stream winding its way south.

I also learned a little about myself and my passion for writing and fishing. Much like writing a book takes time, the same holds true for a new kind of fishing. It takes new equipment and techniques, and sometimes an uncomfortable learning curve. This learning and the challenges that come with it are the reasons my wife and I have a commitment to travel and try new things as much as we can. They are also proof there is still much to be learned about ourselves, one cabin at a time.

Weister Creek

Hard to be a stone
harder still to be a river
held in place by stones.

I had a work-related conference in Eau Claire for a couple of days in April of 2019. Donna tagged along as we'd planned to make a mini-vacation out of it by scheduling a two-night stay at the Kickapoo Valley Ranch after the conference. The Kickapoo ranch was located near La Farge, in the heart of the driftless region of Wisconsin. All it would take to get there would be a detour south into the hills on our way home.

The driftless region of Southwestern Wisconsin is a landscape of stunning beauty, a hidden gem among the expansive cornfields and pasturelands of the Dairy State. Its hills, coulees and valleys are cut by freshwater streams and rivers making it a tourist and trout fishing mecca.

As we entered the fringe of the area, the hills and valleys were lush and green in every direction. Highway 131 cut through it like a two-lane roller-coaster through the most idyllic landscape imaginable. Lovely trout streams followed the road at times, then bent away into the valley pastures. Cows and horses grazed lazily among the stumps and rocky outcrops left behind during the glacial age.

We were quickly reminded this was Amish country as we spotted occasional horse-drawn plows directed by bearded men in wide-brimmed hats. I've always admired the Amish lifestyle. I can't help but think the world might be a better place if we adopted some of the precepts of community. Simplicity and caring for the land are foundational to Amish culture. I see it in Mennonite populations of New York where my wife grew up as well. The minimalist nature of it all drew me in, at least from the comfort of my SUV speeding down the highway. I realize this thinking is in direct conflict with my own life choices as I listened to the on-board navigation system in my climate-controlled Honda. But a guy can dream, can't he?

We arrived at the Kickapoo Valley Ranch mid-afternoon. The entrance led past a fenced-in animal yard that included some sheep and llamas. As we approached, the entire herd of llamas stared with curiosity. Being city folk, both Donna and I were enamored by the awkwardly unique creatures. They have an endearing, safe look to them that makes them appear almost cuddly. I'd heard though, they were known for spitting when threatened, so I kept my distance.

We checked in with Cowboy Joe, one of the proprietors. He and his partner Cowboy David are gracious hosts, and we were soon to find out David is a fantastic baker. He runs a bakery business that serves both local restaurants and the ranch cabins. As a welcome gift, when we arrived in our unit, we found two of his scrumptious cowboy cookies set out on the counter. They were a welcome treat after a long ride in the car.

We unloaded our bags and settled into our cozy cabin. It was one of eight perched on a hillside. Each structure was named after a cowboy character. The owners were inspired by a trip to a ranch out west and decided to create a little of the wild-west experience here in the coulees of the driftless area. Ours was named Slick's Joint, and others were given names like Crazy Jack's Place and Miss Kitty's Rendezvous. The names lent an air of fun about the whole resort.

Once we were settled in, Donna told me if I wanted to go fishing, she would stay back and read her book. There is nothing that gives her more pleasure than sitting alone for hours at a time reading a book and occasionally checking her phone. Books are her passion and escape. One might even say reading is one of her hobbies.

Of course, I jumped at her offer. I love to fish as much as she loves to read, so her suggestion was a win-win proposition. I quickly threw on a long-sleeved shirt, grabbed my fishing rod and tackle, then scrambled out the door.

The driftless area is fly-fishing country, with over 13,000 miles of designated trout streams and rivers winding throughout the picturesque valley lowlands of southwestern Wisconsin. It is truly a treasure.

Now, a full disclosure is in order. As I mentioned previously, I am not a fly fisherman. I have never owned a fly rod, though I do intend to change that in retirement. I have always fished with run-of-the-mill spinning equipment and, until a few years ago, never specifically for trout. I have always considered fly fishermen to be a cut above the rest of us who stick to using simpler spinning rods. Fly fishing requires lots of special equipment including long unwieldy rods with expensive reels. Casting involves lots of whipping and the release of altogether too much line slack during the process. Furthermore, the casting is done in moving water, facilitated by chest or hip waders and a good feel for navigating the slippery stream bottom. It is an art form, for sure.

My luck in Hancock in 2018 made me determined to try my luck at Kickapoo Ranch, so I crossed the county highway from the cabins and walked over to the stream. Near as I could tell, I had the whole section to myself, as far as the eye could see. This section of stream had recently been restored to enhance the trout habitat and improve access for fisherpersons. Cowboy Joe said prior to that effort, the stream was so overgrown it was barely accessible. Based on what I saw, I'd have to offer kudos to the folks at trout Unlimited for what looked like a spectacular job.

Weister Creek bent and wound through lowland pastures spread out in hues of green. In all directions, out buildings dotted the landscape and cows lowed and grazed. As I approached the creek, it babbled in every sense of the word, splashing over rocks strategically placed by the restoration crew. The water was no more than a couple feet deep in most places and appeared to be easily accessible from the banks, which was key, as I had no waders.

On the banks I started fishing near a small bridge that spanned the creek. I'd chosen my ultralight rod and reel. My son had given me the reel for Christmas that year and I was anxious to try it out. My lure of choice was a very small spinner with a bit of deer hair. I approached the whole affair with great skepticism. Much like my muskie outings, I was fully prepared for disappointment. My trout fishing experience in Lanesboro a few years earlier lagged in my mind and served to remind me, with effort, trout could be had.

The stream ran from west to east and the water seemed to be at a decent level, not too high or low. There were obvious cutouts in the embankment, evidence of much higher, faster-moving water, but it appeared those days were past, and I was in luck. Fishing in high water can be difficult. As

I scanned the water it made me think of one of my favorite lines from the classic Richard Brautigan book, *Trout Fishing in America*. The line reads: "The creek was like 12,845 telephone booths in a row with high Victorian ceilings, the doors taken off and the backs of the booths taken out. Sometimes when I went fishing in there, I felt just like a telephone repairman, even though I did not look like one." The mastery of Brautigan!

I cast my spinner toward the middle of the creek and reeled it in. The water was crystalline, making it easy to spot things to be avoided like branches and rocks. Snags are a fisherperson's nemesis and can make an outing maddeningly difficult. At least with trout the hooks are small, making most snags easy to release.

I cast half a dozen times with no sign of anything following my line. If there was one thing I'd learned from the advice of those who'd fished this species before, it was that trout are easily spooked. My first adjustment was to move twenty yards downstream. As with most fishing, if the action is slow at a location, it's time to move along.

I found a nice bend where a slow-moving eddy swirled in a circle. Again, I am no trout expert, but the eddy seemed like a good location for a fish to take a much-needed break from the swift current of the stream. I threw my spinner into the eddy and immediately felt a little tug on the ultralight rod. These rods are short, thin and highly sensitive, making small catches easily detectable and large ones a fun challenge. I gave the line a slight tug to set the hook and continued my retrieve. The pull of the current worked against me, giving the fish an additional advantage in its quest to free itself.

I reeled quickly as the small fish zigged and zagged in resistance. I pulled the little guy to shore, a beautifully colored Brown Trout. It was small, no more than a seven incher, with a golden underbelly and a series of bright red dots along its side. This truly was a fish of a different color. I've caught numerous species in my life, but this certainly had to be the most beautiful, from a coloring standpoint, anyway.

I was absolutely giddy. It was fairly amazing how much pride a seven-inch catch can well-up in a seasoned fisherman. In any freshwater lake, a fish of this size would be laughed at, scorned and tossed back in shame. However, at this stream, using unconventional equipment for the task, this little creature brought me an unexpected sense of pride. In essence, I'd scaled a different face of the same mountain. The daunting mystique of trout fishing suddenly felt lighter and more penetrable. I was simply elated with myself.

I snapped a picture as proof of my catch and quickly set the fish free. I moved downstream and continued my quest to see if I could turn a good day into a better one. The idyllic setting of stream, farmland and fresh air were only offset by a vicious and zealous population of black flies. They bit and buzzed with fury, taking my concentration away from my casting and turning it to minimizing the number of bites to my noggin. As I moved down the stream, each new location seemed to get me a new fish and after two and a half hours I'd caught and released half a dozen Brown and Rainbow Trout.

I was happy with my production for the day. I'd started out hoping to catch a single trout so catching six was much better than I expected. I would have stayed longer, but two and a half hours of slapping at black flies pretty much took away my will to live, let alone my zest for the elusive trout. I'd had enough fun for the day, and in the process proved my skill to myself, if no one else. I fastened my lure to the cork on the rod and headed back up to the cabin feeling grateful and accomplished.

*   *   *

As we've grown old together, my wife and I have redis-covered some of ourselves and, in a sense, regained our identities. Our empty nest has brought forth interests and gifts that were waylaid during the childrearing years. My love for words and the entire writing process has developed into an obsession. My new preoccupation with the craft is not entirely healthy, but one I've come to honor as part of my life's path.

Similarly, Donna has fallen deeply back into love with books and quiet time alone. The two of us can sit in a room for hours doing these separate things with complete respect for the others' pursuits. There is a satisfying comfort that comes with sitting in silence in the same room with someone you've spent the last 30 years with. It is our love language.

Much of the rest of our two-night stay was spent doing just these things – we read, wrote and relaxed. Whether it was on our deck overlooking the lush greenery of the hills and valleys, or inside stretched out on our separate chairs. Some might see this as a dull vacation, but much of the reason we were there was to slow down and just chill.

This is not to say we didn't do anything else. We drove to the nearby town of Viroqua on our second day and cel-ebrated our anniversary with dinner at the Driftless Café. This little gem of a restaurant was worth every mile of the ride. The organic prairie beef tenderloin I had was simply off-the-charts delicious. The café specializes in farm-to-table cuisine that is almost entirely locally grown. The place was packed and buzzing with diners as excited as we were to be part of this corporate culinary orgasm. We finished with a dessert of flourless chocolate cake with raspberry puree that was the perfect ending to a perfect meal. If we ate like that every night, we would both weigh 300 pounds, but it sure felt nice to splurge. It was exquisite!

After dinner, we drove back to the ranch and sat on our front porch watching the sunset. As we did, a cow moseyed up the twisting gravel drive leading up to the cabin area. It plodded along like it was on some sort of covert cow mission. The beast took all the turns that the fencing and gravel defined for it, not really knowing where it led. We laughed expecting farmer McDougal to come along at any minute and ask us if we'd seen a cow around anywhere.

"Yep. Just wandered up the drive that way, sir."

We never really saw a resolution to the lost Holstein. I suppose someone eventually figured out they were one cow short of a herd and went looking for her. Or maybe farmers tag them with GPS nowadays. I'm not sure. It was simply a momentary source of amusement for us. This kind of thing would probably make the headlines in the local newspaper.

In the end, I can't say enough about the charm of the Kickapoo Valley Ranch. If you're looking for a complete getaway with lots of quiet, occasionally punctuated by the clip-clop of a horse-drawn Amish wagon, then this place is for you. Like many of our cabin experiences, the minute we arrived, our blood pressure dropped ten points. For us mid-lifers, it was restorative and rejuvenating. When it comes to relaxing, calming getaway vacations, I was glad we drifted into the driftless area.

Lake Napowan

Watching from the dock
how delicately the dragonfly lands
on the damp lily pad.

As the kids grew older and took on the challenges of college and part time jobs, family gatherings at the lake were harder to come by. Summers in Wisconsin are short, and Donna and I have grown to love life at the cabin, so when the itch hits, she starts browsing the available places on HomeAway and VRBO. In 2017, she discovered some friends of ours owned an A-frame cabin outside of Wild Rose, Wisconsin. They offered to give us a significant discount, so we booked a date to go with our friends, Steve and Jill.

Lake Napowan was a short two-and-a-half-hour drive from our house in Waukesha. We've discovered after spending so many years driving five hours or more to get to our cabin on Spider Lake in Mercer, there are plenty to be found at less than a three-hour drive. I'm still a firm believer that the best environment is found in the far north, north of Wausau in Wisconsin, or north of Brainerd, in Minnesota. But from a quick getaway standpoint, places like Lake Napowan are perfect.

We arrived at the cabin before Jill and Steve. In a matter of minutes, we were unpacked and toured the place. It was the perfect size for two couples. The living area was open concept with a high, vaulted ceiling accented by two huge windows at the second story level. These windows allowed elegant rays of natural light into the main rooms. The woodwork was a light-colored knotty pine giving the place an up-north feel, yet tastefully modern. A couple of fans hung from the high ceiling to push the heat down in the winter and move the air in summer.

When we were unpacked, I told Donna I was going down to the dock to fish. I said it was my goal to catch one and text a picture to Steve before he got there. We routinely exchange friendly banter about the first catch, plus I knew it would provide him some incentive to step on the gas and get there quicker.

I grabbed a beer and my fishing rod and walked down the stepped path to the dock. The lake was small and fairly shallow, at least as far as the dock extended. I set down my beer and started casting. Like every cabin I've been to, I felt my blood pressure drop immediately. A calm settled in and the worries of my job, mortgage and car repairs began to melt away. The light breeze off the lake, the fragrance of the pines with just a hint of wood smoke combined to create a balm of serenity and peace. The silence was positively deafening. Cabin life is the good life, and if you can get it, you should. I was grateful my wife had reached out to our friends to book this stay.

On my fourth or fifth cast, I felt a tug on my line. I set the hook and reeled in a small bass. I unhooked it, snapped a picture and let it go. I sent the photo to Steve and mentioned he owed me five bucks. It's a running joke we have. When we're fishing with my kids, I always say, "First fish gets five bucks from Uncle Steve." It drives him crazy. Our teasing and mutual insults are part of what makes fishing together so much fun.

The next two days were spent fishing, relaxing with cocktails on the deck, and eating lots of good food. My wife is a phenomenal cook, and meal planning for these kinds of trips is one of her superpowers. We ate and drank like kings and queens, because everyone knows calories and diets take vacations at the same time we do. Life is too short to worry about anything at the cabin.

Steve and I did our fair share of fishing on Napowan. It is a fun lake if you're into catching a couple dozen thirteen-inch bass. We both love any action on the water, so we took what we could get and made the best of it.

In the evening of our second day, the four of us took a "booze cruise" around the lake. Steve set the trolling motor to a casual two miles per hour and linked his Bluetooth speaker to his phone for some music. We slowly moved around the lake, laughing and telling stories. Contrary to my core belief, just because we were in a boat didn't mean we had to be fishing. There is something to be said for a little downtime on the water while at the lake.

We glided around taking in the local wildlife. A family of ducks swam along the shoreline, fish jumped stretching for bugs on the water's surface and dragonflies flitted around us on their journey to somewhere else. The highlight though, was a great blue heron we saw feeding in the distant reeds. I realize these birds are more common than I think, but they always catch my breath when I see one in the water. They are amazingly graceful birds with all their attendant awkwardness. With their long, skinny legs and oversized bills for catching fish, they look like a bird put together by committee. They look prehistoric yet possess an evolved sort of beauty. Jill, who loves photography, snapped several photos with her phone of the bird as we slowly passed by.

The whole evening was a mellow kind of chill. It felt good to be with our friends of over 25 years, talking about our lives and just enjoying each other's presence on our working-class yacht.

We went up to the Napowan cabin again the following year because we'd had such a good time. The place was a pleasant reminder that, as we reached the latter stages of middle age, we didn't have to pack for ourselves *and* the kids and drive half a day to get to a place of relaxation and renewal. In this case, our friends were much like family anyway, and their presence was filling the absence of our kids. It is nearly impossible to have a bad time at the lake, and when it is shared with good friends it becomes exponentially more fun.

Lake Arbutus

Fishing on the reef
waves lift and drop each boat
like a metronome.

The year 2020 will go down as one of the most tumultuous years in the history of this country and, for that matter, the world. COVID-19 began its spread into the United States in January, and by March the country began shutting down as people navigated the global pandemic. People were forced to work and school from home in virtual environments. Most of us were not familiar with or prepared for all of the sudden disruption in our day to day living.

Added to this was the murder of George Floyd in the Twin Cities and all the subsequent civil unrest. During the protests and related rioting, I feared for my daughter's safety. She and her boyfriend lived just a couple of miles from the epicenter of the violence and because my wife and I lived three hundred miles away, there was nothing we could do but hope and pray.

Throw into the mix a number of mass shootings, protests, the false claims of a rigged election and its resulting insurrection on our nation's capital, and it added up to civil and social unrest at a level we haven't seen since the '60s. For months there was nothing we could do but wear a mask, wash our hands, stay at home and sit within our misery and fear.

A pandemic and all that our country was going through served to spark my wife and me to reprioritize what is important in life. The biggest takeaway for her and I was, nothing is more important than time spent with family. For months our contact with Sarah and Ben was minimal. In an effort to salvage something from the "lost summer," Donna started looking for a cabin somewhere between the Twin Cities and Waukesha. After a little searching, she found a place near Black River Falls, Wisconsin. There were enough bedrooms to accommodate all five of us including Sarah's boyfriend, Sam, so she booked a stay for three days and two nights in August.

The agreement was, we would all get COVID-19 tests before we met, just to be sure. We wanted to do the right thing, knowing if we didn't, we were part of the problem. After all, there was plenty of judgment and shame being spread when people posted something about their travel on social media outlets, and we wanted to avoid that scorn. All of us had been extremely vigilant in our safety throughout the pandemic to this point. We also knew there was a small chance of becoming infected between the time of our tests and when we met, but to be sure we all agreed to quarantine between the test and the trip. It was unanimous the effort to see each other was worth the risk. We were all tired and missed the company of one another. The tradition of family time at a cabin needed to continue.

* * *

We picked up Ben in Madison around 11 a.m. and headed west. Sarah and Sam had a shorter drive so mentioned they would be leaving a little after us. When we picked Ben up, we both gave him a long overdue hug.

"So, how are you doing?" Donna asked.

"Okay, I guess. Kinda tired."

"How's it going with your roommates?"

"Mom, don't get me started. They are so messy. Being cooped up hasn't helped. I can't wait to get a place of my own."

"Well, it'll be nice to get away for a few days, right?" I asked.

"Exactly. I'm looking forward to the quiet."

Outside of Black River Falls, I mentioned to Donna that I wanted to stop and get some nightcrawlers for fishing. I worked my way downtown and parked on the main drag at a hardware store advertising live bait. I put on my face mask assuming the store required them for staff and customers.

I walked in and was greeted by an unmasked clerk.

"Hello! What can I help you with today?"

The gentleman seemed nice enough and non-judgmental, but I kept my distance anyway.

"Hi, I'm looking for nightcrawlers."

"Back corner of the store, by the sporting goods."

"Thank you, sir," I replied.

I walked in the direction he'd pointed. When I got to the sporting goods area, I was surprised to find a half a dozen people, all unmasked, at the gun and ammunition counter. When I entered, a number of them turned and gawked at me, the masked marauder in search of fat worms. Now, I am a fairly self-conscious person. I'm the guy who doesn't like to wear shirts with logos or sayings for fear of attracting unwanted attention. I am a big fan of blending in. Here I was in a crowd of gun customers in a conservative small town wearing one of those government-mandated masks. If I'd been wearing a pink spandex leotard, I might have fit in better than I did with that mask on my face.

I tried to look casual as I wandered around looking for a small refrigerator that might hold the bait and essentially free me from the scorn of the locals. As I searched, I speculated as to why there was a run on guns at the store on this day. Parts of the country were still burning from the social unrest, and, for some reason, the fear was stoking gun sales across America. Ammunition was scarce and people seemed to think the best answer to violence was to be locked and loaded to create more if it came to their part of the country.

Me? I just wanted some worms to help my kids catch some fish.

A few minutes of aimless wandering later, I finally found the bait cooler and picked up what I'd come for. I asked the friendly clerk how the fishing had been at Lake Arbutus, and he said he hadn't heard much about that particular lake.

"But, hey, good luck anyway!" he said.

"Thanks again," I said as I paid him and left.

* * *

The cabin was off the main highway down a gravel driveway. It was a two-story structure and had the appearance and feel of a house. It was a newer construction and featured a concrete patio area on the east end with a number of chairs and loungers set out to enjoy the late summer sun.

The interior was spacious and modern. A bookcase on one wall held a plethora of books for guests to read in case the weather didn't cooperate. One of the noticeable quirks of the main room was the large overhead garage door. It seemed it was designed to be able to close off the eastern facing windows during winter months to add a layer of insulation and protection from the winter winds. The owner acknowledged the door was slated to be removed in a future renovation.

Donna, Ben and I unloaded the car and took a walk down to the lake to check out the water. The grounds were spacious and well-maintained. I peeked in their equipment shed and found a couple of stand-up paddle boards and kayaks. They were not fishing kayaks like I was used to, but I figured I could make them work. I knew my kids wanted to fish, and between the kayaks and a canoe in the pole barn, it looked like we had enough boats, so that was good.

Within forty-five minutes, Sarah and Sam pulled into the driveway. We greeted them with hugs, happy to be back together after not seeing one another since Christmas. When kids reach the age of independence, new jobs and apartments, you appreciate your time together even more. It is a mixed blessing to watch them make their way as adults and eventually come to the point where they don't really need their parents like they once did. I know that is what parenting is all about, but it's just bittersweet sometimes.

We spent the afternoon lounging around, snacking and catching up with one another. Sarah and Sam described their summer of protests and riots in Minneapolis, and both were glad to be out of the city for a while. Sarah and I both tried our hand at fishing from the dock but had no luck. The lake had a sandy bottom and was fairly shallow, making it less than ideal for fish.

That night we had dinner and celebrated Ben's twenty-second birthday with chocolate cupcakes for dessert. He was preparing for his last semester at UW-Madison, with full expectation it would probably be a mix of in-person and virtual instruction. He too was grateful to be away from the city and his four college roommates. It seemed everyone needed a break from the cloak of COVID-19.

After dinner, I was itching to get out and do a little fishing in one of the kayaks. No one else was interested, so I grabbed my gear and headed to the equipment shed. Once I'd launched the kayak, a couple things became quite clear. First, this was certainly not the fishing kayak I owned back home, and second, I *really* liked my kayak. This was a sit-on-top model which was much less conducive to fishing. But like many things when you're at the cabin, you kind of make the best of what you have. Sometimes it's a spatula from 1969, other times it's a sit-on-top kayak.

I paddled in the direction of the nearest set of reeds I could see. When I arrived, I cast furiously with my go-to lure that worked like a dream on the smallmouth bass back home. It took significant effort, but I finally got a strike. I set the hook with glee, knowing I would not go home skunked. More importantly, I had identified a potential spot for the kids the following night. I've come to the point in my life where it is as much a thrill for me to watch other people catch fish. If I am an instigator of that, well, even better.

The fish fought with the trademark fight of a smallmouth bass. Pound for pound, they are the best fighters out there. It put up a spunky battle, but I prevailed and pulled the 12-incher over the side. It would have been an insignificant catch on any other outing, but any time I'm trying out a new, untested lake and actually catch something, well, that fish becomes significant.

I managed to catch three more just like it within the next half hour and then the bite shut down again. It was a gorgeous sunset, and I didn't want to be on the lake after dark with no lights, so I paddled back to the cabin. I walked in to find the kids playing a board game while Donna read her book. It was heartwarming to see them playing together like they had done so many years ago as much smaller kids. No pandemic, no riots, no work or school stress. Just board games and a beer. I washed up and wandered over to the game table.

"Catch anything, Dad?" Sarah asked.

"Yeah, actually. I think I found a spot we can try tomorrow night. Caught a few smallmouths. No real size, but still fun."

"Cool. Sam and I definitely want to go," She replied.

"Yeah, me too, Dad," Ben added.

It felt good to have kids that wanted to fish, who I didn't feel were doing it only to appease me. Those days spent on the dock ducking from flying hooks and taking fish off as fast as they were caught, had paid lifelong dividends.

* * *

The next day was spent swimming, sharing meals and hanging out at the cabin. I took an exploratory trek out on the trail leading from the back yard. It ended at the Hatfield dam that served to create the flowage forming Lake Arbutus. The dam was built on the Black River as a source of hydroelectric power and, when the water behind it is released, serves as a source of recreation for white water enthusiasts down river.

The dam exposes a long stretch of what was once river bottom below it. Here the river bottom is made up of large boulders of gneiss, a volcanic rock believed to be over 2.8 billion years old. These rocks triggered my inner twelve-year-old and I couldn't resist. There were signs on the dam warning of the danger of potential water releases. A large alarm horn and warning lights on the side of the structure made me trepidatious. Nevertheless, I couldn't hold myself back from doing a little boulder climbing.

I climbed down the embankment and started picking my way over the bedrock one sure-footed step at a time. I've twisted my ankle enough in my life to know how treacherous these rocks can be, and I certainly didn't want to tweak one on vacation. With my height, it helped having legs like a human stork to make some of the more challenging drops and rises a little more manageable.

I might add, there is something spiritual about being among rocks almost 3 billion years old. It is not unlike being among the Sequoias of northern California. These natural formations instill a sense of wonder and majesty in me. They are also reminders of the smallness and insignificance of our humanity. They whisper that our time here on this borrowed planet is better spent in appreciation of such things, rather than their exploitation.

After a bit of climbing, I found a flat rock and sat for a bit. I took advantage of the solitude and just sat meditatively thinking about everything and nothing. I reflected on how lucky I was to have the family I loved so much. These moments hanging out with them away from the global plague and civil unrest was grounding for me, and I think the same held true for them. In times of trouble and uncertainty, the best thing for everyone is to rally around loved ones and huddle-up. With our urban environments in various stages of chaos and anarchy, this natural world to which we retreated provided a much-needed balm. So, I laid there and thought about such things. It was a Buddhist-like Zen in the midst of a world on fire.

* * *

That night after a delicious meal, we all portaged the boats down to the lake for an evening of fishing. Ben and I each took a kayak and Sarah and Sam took the canoe. A year earlier they had kayaked together up at Pine Forest Lodge, but as we all know, canoeing is a different beast. Paddling together should be a required compatibility test of all couples considering a long-term relationship. It requires patience and teamwork and usually ends up with one of three outcomes; gentle encouragement of one another, laughter and lighthearted fun, or a screaming, raging conflict. In a canoe, every couple falls somewhere along this spectrum.

As they moved along, Sarah and Sam fell somewhere between the encouragement and the laughter. It made my heart happy. They were not only on the water doing some fishing, but they were working out their teamwork in the canoe together. I wasn't sure what the future held for these two, but she seemed to have found a good one. They were a nice match.

We all paddled out to my lucky spot from the day before. We cast our lines near the reeds several times, to no avail. Sarah and Sam had trouble keeping their position, as is often the case with canoe fishing. Both they and Ben, moved on to the next set of reeds hoping to find better luck.

Eventually, I moved on as well. After an hour and a half of futility between the four of us, we all started back home. Despite being skunked, we got to enjoy a stunning sunset together. The thing about fishing is, you can't catch them if you don't try. Sometimes there is fun, and beauty and laughter built into the effort of trying. All I knew was, it felt good to be together with my kids doing the thing I'd taught them to love. And, as the saying goes, we'll get 'em next time.

* * *

When we got back to the cabin, Sarah asked if we wanted to play a board game. She is an absolute board game fanatic, and loves the long, epic games of strategy and skill. Most of them require knowledge of an extensive set of rules and sub-rules. There are usually a million pieces and two decks of strategy cards that go with them. When I was a young person, it was Monopoly and Life, and the only "hard" game of strategy was Risk. That was it.

Be clear, I do not judge her or other board game aficionados, in fact I respect them. I admire their ability to come around a table and have fun, all while planning, plotting and using their brain for something other than staring at a screen. It is actually quite refreshing. When I joked with her about her Tupperware bins full of games, she said, "It could be worse Dad. It could be drugs."

I had to agree. She certainly had a point.

Donna and I have a difficult time with the more complex games Sarah plays. The two of us have trouble keeping track of the multiple layers of rules and understanding the long-range strategies of each. So, when Sarah asked if we wanted to play a game, we told her as long as it was simple, fun, and didn't take two hours to finish.

"Okay, I've got a good one for you. It's called: Stay Cool," she said.

"Simple and short?" I asked.

"Yeah. It's really fun. It's a multitasking game."

She set things up and explained the rules. It involved an "active player" who is peppered with questions from two different people reading from cards. One of the questions must be answered verbally, but the other must be spelled out using the seven dice with letters on them. All of this is happening while a sand timer is used to track time. The time element makes the stress of answering two questions even more stressful. Believe me when I say it is harder than it sounds.

We started the game, and the laughter began almost immediately. Watching people struggle to try and do two things at once requiring separate parts of their brain, as well as fine motor skills, was highly entertaining. When my turn rolled around, I found it frustrating and nerve-wracking. One of the rules requires the person reading the question to repeat it if the active player is focused on their other task. Add to this the egg timer factor and the stage is set for fun, mostly for the ones watching and asking the questions.

In a way, the game was a flashback to my days as a young father. Here I had both of my kids asking questions at the same time and each demanding an answer. If I delayed in answering one or the other, they asked again. The exercise certainly gave justification for why the game was named "Stay Cool." It was certainly good advice for the players of it as well as an apt piece of advice for young parenthood.

* * *

Mornings at the cabin were for Donna and me. While the kids slept in, we occupied ourselves by reading, writing and catching up with social media. I've grown to love the quiet of mornings, especially for writing, as my mind is clear and relatively free from the worries and thoughts that come throughout the day.

On the Sunday we were to leave, I perused the books on the owner's shelves to see if there were any that caught my eye. I had finished journaling for the morning and was looking for something to read. I came across Annie Dillard's book, *The Writing Life*. Having just spent the last hour penning my thoughts, I pulled the book out for a look. What I found were words of incredible poetic beauty about the process of sitting down and writing a story. I've read many books about the craft, but never one quite as poetically descriptive about the challenges and rewards putting pen to paper can bring.

As I turned through the first few pages, I fell in love with her style. She had a way of using her words like an artist uses oils on a canvas. The result was almost breathtaking.

I consider finding these kinds of treasures one of the fringe benefits of time spent at any cabin. Years ago, my brother Paul gave me a book by J. Maarten Troost titled: *The Sex Lives of Cannibals.* He said he'd started it when he'd found it on the shelves up at Pine Forest Lodge.

"It's a hilarious book, Jim. I thought of you when I was reading it. Give it a read and when you're back up at the cabin next, just leave it up there," he said.

The book was so good, I went on to read all the other books Troost had written, mostly about his travels to extreme places. When I finished, I left it back up at the cabin for someone else to discover maybe next month, or maybe 10 years from now. As I said, part of the whole cabin experience is coming across gems like these among the stacks of aging Readers Digest Condensed books and old Stephen King novels. Because there's nothing like a good book to read at the lake.

* * *

Before we left for home on Sunday we took a side-trip to Wazee Lake. It is a nearby park that features a man-made lake formed by an abandoned taconite quarry that filled in over time. It is now the deepest non-natural lake in the state and serves as a great training ground for scuba divers and recreational paddlers. It was a nice hike down to the water's edge and a good way to stretch our legs before the long ride home.

At the shore we took some time to rest at a picnic table and have a light lunch. When we were done, we hiked back to the cars. We shared hugs with each other as we wished Sarah and Sam safe travels for their trip back to the Twin Cities. We'd had a fantastic getaway and I was sad to see it come to an end.

This trip with the kids to Lake Arbutus filled a space for all of us, a chasm dug into our psyches by a global pandemic. Each of us had our own COVID-19 trauma to sift through and escape from for a few days. It wasn't until we were away from it, removed to the relative safety of woods and water, that we were able to step back and assess the state of ourselves and one another. Being pent up in homes and apartments for months on end can change a person. It puts into perspective what's important. It gives a person pause for self-reflection, introspection and, if so led, a chance to mourn and grieve what once was.

Being at the lake together gave all of us the break from routine we needed to propel us into fall and eventually a dark winter of even more seclusion and solitude. It felt as if the life-giving energy of the woods and water was drawn into our bodies and souls accompanied by a whisper of "It's okay. You're going to be fine."

This life-restoring energy of nature, alongside high-quality time spent with family is what draws us back every year. It is what drew Mom to take us to the cabin in Hibbing over fifty years ago. When I think back over it all, the fish, the boat trips, swimming beach escapades, barbecues and most of all, the long and winding conversations with family and friends over coffee or beer, I get wistful. Life at the lake is a little piece of perfection we build into our lives every year to remind us to slow down, listen to our souls, and appreciate those around us. It is why we will continue to go back. Because it has become part of who we are.

Acknowledgments

I'd like to thank a few folks who made this book possible. First and foremost, to my wife, Donna, for being such a great support during all my writing pursuits. To say I love you doesn't say enough. I'd also like to thank my kids for their roles as characters in this book. My fondest cabin memories are those that include them. Gratitude to my friends, Arlene and Darlene, for their help in editing and critiques.

To my publisher, Cornerstone Press, thank you for believing in me and taking my words to the greater world. In particular, thank you to publisher Dr. Ross Tangedal, managing editor Brett Hill, and production director Amanda Leibham.

I cannot thank enough my friend, colleague, and fellow poet, Gary Busha, for the use of poems from his collection, *On the Dock* (Wolfsong 2017). His words help set the stage for the stories told within. When I first met Gary at a poetry conference, he said he wrote Haiku but didn't like the restrictiveness of five-seven-five, so he does his own thing. I love what that taught me about the freedom our art grants us as writers and poets. Thank you, Gary, for your friendship and your poetry.

Gratefully acknowledged are *Portage Magazine* and *Wisconsin Outdoor News*, where small portions of this book appeared in earlier forms.

JIM LANDWEHR is the author of three memoirs, *Cretin Boy*, *Dirty Shirt*, and *The Portland House*. He has also published five poetry collections, *Thoughts from a Line at the DMV*, *Genetically Speaking*, *Reciting from Memory*, *Written Life*, and *On a Road*. His nonfiction has been published in *Main Street Rag*, *The Sun Magazine*, *Story News*, and others. His poetry has been featured in *Rosebud Magazine*, *The Orchards Poetry Journal*, *Blue Heron Review*, and many others. Jim was the 2018–2019 poet laureate for the Village of Wales, Wisconsin. For more on his writing, visit: https://jimlandwehr.com